WHAT THE HELL IS A GROOM AND WHAT'S HE SUPPOSED TO DO?

WHAT THE HELL IS A
GROOM
AND
WHAT'S HE
SUPPOSED
TO DO?

John Mitchell

Andrews McMeel
Publishing

Kansas City

www.andrewsmcmeel.com

98 99 00 01 02 RDH 10 9 8 7 6 5 4 3 2 1

Library of Congress Cataloging-in-Publication Data

Mitchell, John, 1967–
    What the hell is a groom and what's he supposed to do? / John Mitchell.
        p.   cm.
    Includes bibliographical references.
    ISBN 0-8362-7869-0 (pbk.)
    1. Bridegrooms—United States. 2. Weddings—United States—Planning. 3. Wedding etiquette—United States. 4. Etiquette for men—United States. I. Title.
    HQ745.M655   1999
    395.2'2—dc21   98-37652
                                                              CIP

Book design by Holly Camerlinck
Composition by Kelly & Company, Lee's Summit, Missouri

ATTENTION: SCHOOLS AND BUSINESSES

Without a second thought, this book is dedicated to my wonderful wife, Tracey, for our beautiful wedding and our great life together. In many ways, more than the obvious, without her, this book would not have been possible. To her, my wife, my best friend, my confidante and bitching post, my editor and biggest supporter . . . I love you.

I would also like to thank my family, PE on the beach, Darren, Brian, and Tina (and to Donnie, I dedicate a copy of my book . . . nothin' like puttin' on the pressure); and thanks to my in-laws, Ro and Joe, Lou and Mar, David, and Raymie for their support. Thanks as well to my agent, Rhoda Weyr, for her persistence and confidence; and to Jean Zevnik, my editor, and the staff at Andrews McMeel.

CONTENTS

3. WEDDING PLANNING

5. HAPPILY EVER AFTER

6. WORKSHEETS AND RESOURCES

CHAPTER 1

SURVIVAL BASICS

OUT OF DISASTER COMES LOVE

Tracey lost everything. Her TV, her stereo, and all her furniture was destroyed when a pipe burst in the apartment above. She cried for days. At the urging of a friend she decided to visit a local furniture store.

The holidays were pretty slow for John. Three days before Christmas, shoppers have a lot of things other than buying furniture on their minds. In keeping with the holiday spirit, John decided to let his salespeople leave early that evening. He would cover the sales floor himself, an unusual occurrence for the owner.

Late that cold, wintry night Tracey visited the store. Tracey and John chatted, flirted a little, and found that they had a lot in common. Three hours later Tracey had a new sleeper sofa, cocktail and end tables, lamps, pictures, and fabric protection, and John had . . . a date.

Five years later, Tracey says John took advantage of a vulnerable female in distress. John says Tracey bought everything in the store but *he's* been paying for it ever since!

They have been happily married for three years.

ESPECIALLY FOR THE LADIES

Future brides . . . this is a guys' book. There are literally hundreds of books and thousands of magazines discussing the details of wedding planning from the bride's perspective. So, with all that information already out there for you, why the heck are you reading a book written for men?

I'll tell you why . . . you're engaged now, and "Prince Charming" is turning this happy affair into the *Nightmare on Elm Street, Part 26*. Even though he may have proposed to you, he doesn't seem very excited about getting married. He's been moping around the apartment, acting kind of funny, and seems distracted all the time. You pull out your trusty bridal magazines and books and ask him to look at the pretty pictures with you and he moves to the other side of the couch. He hasn't said too much about the wedding, and he never expresses his feelings to you anymore. One time, he even blew up at you when you simply asked him whether he prefers the pink brides-maids' dresses or the purple ones. You don't understand what the heck is going on with him and why he's acting like this. This should be the happiest and most fun occasion of his life, right?

Whether or not it's actually true, guys like to feel like they are in control, the masters of their domain. During the wedding planning, he may feel like he's only along for the ride and may not really under-stand what's going on or how the wedding process really works. (And ladies, traditionally most of you have been no help whatsoever, and in some cases, many of you have actually aggravated the situation.)

You think to yourself, "I don't understand. I'm totally supportive of my future husband." Well, think about it. You went off on your own and discussed the wedding plans with your mother and friends and even with his mother. He's only peripherally included in these discussions. You are constantly on the phone with your girlfriends planning the pending nuptials while your fiancé sits on the couch looking like a lump. You try to include him in your discussions and sometimes you ask for his opinion, but he acts like he doesn't care. The reason is, he probably doesn't really understand what's going on, what's expected of him, or how the whole bloody wedding process works because no one ever told him. This isn't a football game, and he didn't grow up watching the Dallas Cowgirls All Dressed in White versus the New York Giant Flower Arrangements play for the world championship of weddings. It's safe to assume he doesn't know the wedding-planning rules. You treat the wedding like an "all-girls club" . . . no guys allowed. Except, ladies, you really do need us. You can't expect him to be interested in the wedding when you keep pushing bridal magazines in his face and asking him to look at pictures of dresses. As macho as he thinks he is, looking at dresses and actually talking about them can be intimidating to him. Guys usually don't feel comfortable asking their mother or friends how this wedding thing works. It's just not in our nature. We feel stupid. It's an unwritten code among guys: Don't ask, don't tell. He's really not as insensitive as you think he is. He's probably very confused and overwhelmed, but he really does care.

It's up to you, ladies. The proverbial ball is in your court. Throughout this book I will be sympathetic to your wedding-planning cause and always give *you,* the fiancée, the bride, and the future wife, the benefit of the doubt. This book teaches him to always consider you first. So ladies, work with us guys. Even though we seem like the enemy, we're not. We really do want to be involved in our wedding planning. Read through the book. Understand his perspective and respect that perspective. Because Lord knows, this book hammers your wishes into his head. What the hell, maybe you can even make him feel like he's "in control"? (We all know better though.)

This unique book not only highlights many of the topics that affect both of you but will also help you understand his perspective as well. The guy's perspective will give you the insight necessary so that you will be able to teach your fiancé how to become "interested" and active in the wedding planning. Have fun and have a happy, wonderful wedding.

Even if you don't read through the entire book make sure you take the time to read the "Right of First Refusal" section and sign the "Right of First Refusal" Pledge at the back of the book. It can save both of you plenty of heartache and stress.

FOR THE GUYS

So you want to get married. You've found the girl of your dreams and you're making the big jump from having a girlfriend to having a fiancée to having a wife. That's a mouthful for such little words. It will be an adventure, terrifying at times, but well worth the trip.

We are at a crossroads to a new millennium. Guys today are liberated, right? We are sensitive and in touch with our feminine side. We occasionally help our fiancée clean up, a little. We take out the garbage, sometimes. We throw in a load of laundry, every once in a while. We wash her car and get her the new muffler she needs. And yes, we are capable of being romantic; we sometimes even microwave that "Hungry Man" dinner for two. *Guys unite. We want to be a part of our wedding planning, damn it!*

Hopefully, you are reading this book well before you get engaged, since I'm about to make your life much easier. I have devoted a whole section to the formal engagement. But, like most guys, you probably didn't plan ahead and are reading this book as a last resort to understand the ever-increasing complexity and madness of preparing for a wedding. That's okay; all's not lost. It's never too late.

You're not alone. Every year more than two million guys in the United States get married, and most live to tell about it. Hell, if a dumb ex-jock like me could survive it, anyone can. Right now it may seem overwhelming, but don't worry; it gets worse. This book will give you an insight into what to expect and what you are required to do, as well as offering general observations on wedding protocol. We will explore the proposal, the engagement, the actual planning of the wedding, the big day, the honeymoon, and the trials and tribulations of life eternally after marriage. In Chapter 6, I have provided you with checklists, worksheets, and other resources to help you on your way and keep you organized.

The advice you will find in this book is the same advice I would give my brother. I only wish I'd had a guy to explain how this whole damn thing worked when we were planning our wedding. Enough of the dress-and-flower crap. I'm here, guys—you can count on me to lead you through the minefield. I'm going to be your coach. I will instruct you in all the finer points of planning a wedding. Now, hit the ground and give me twenty. After you have done your twenty, read on.

I did most of your homework for you. I read dozens of wedding books, hundreds of magazines, and talked with numerous couples before and after my wedding. Most books and articles are geared toward the bride. Yeah, some may throw us guys a bone, but not many. I don't think many guys have much use for "Helpful Hints for Hair and Nail Care," "How to Deal with Your PMS," "Choosing the Gown That's Right for You," or "Your Wedding Lingerie and Trousseau."

BELIEVE IT OR NOT, THE WEDDING-PLANNING PROCESS IS QUITE SIMILAR TO PLAYING BALL:

Having A Girlfriend ➤ Playing ball in the backyard with local kids. Nothing serious, nothing organized.

Getting Engaged ➤ You have now officially signed up and are on the team.

Wedding Planning ➤ Team practice. Just like your coach said, "Practice the way you play." Drill over and over so that you have the perfect game. Make sure you have all bases covered.

Rehearsal Dinner ➤ Pregame drills. Walk-through. You're ready for the big game.

The Wedding ➤ The Big Show. The Super Bowl. The World Series. The World Cup. The Olympics.

Reception ➤ Your victory party.

Honeymoon ➤ Time off after the championship game. Your chance to relax and unwind before you begin your daily routine again. Just like the pro said, "I'm going to Disney World."

Don't worry: I'm not going to cover anything about your underwear . . . just make sure it's clean!

You have a lot of work ahead of you. It's not easy planning a wedding. You think to yourself, "How complicated can it be? Pick a cake. Select some flowers. Take a few pictures. No problem." Think again. It's just not that easy. In the entire history of the world, no woman has ever been casual about her wedding. Ask your family and friends. A wedding takes a lot more effort and planning than throwing a keg party for the college frat brothers. At times you may become frustrated with the whole thing and think, "Why the hell am I doing this? Is it worth it? Damn, we should have eloped instead!" You may feel like the whole thing is passing you by. Your fiancée seems to be scheming and plotting with both her mother and yours. They don't consult with you about anything and they treat you like a little kid. It can make you feel like you are not even a participant in your own wedding. Every guy goes through this at some point throughout the planning. Stick with it and keep your mouth shut for now!

Think of this as your *Cliffs Notes* of planning a wedding. I address only those parts that apply to you, and explain wedding planning in a clear, concise manner, without all the girlie garbage. It's a quick and dirty explanation of only the important "guy" parts of wedding planning. Inevitably, I'm going to get these la-di-da wedding consultants and so-called experts criticizing my book, simply because I tell it how it is. I don't pooh-pooh the difficult topics or sugarcoat anything. Most of these "planners and experts" are women, and I don't think many of them had sex changes; therefore, they could not possibly know the men's perspective. They will say, "Of course I understand, *IIII* have conducted three gazillion weddings and *IIIII tell* the groom what he wants!" Well, that's not my idea of a personal wedding. I've been there, done that, got the T-shirt. Anyway guys, just do what feels right. And remember, this is just a guide. There are no hard and fast rules . . . no matter what people tell you.

COLD FEET . . . WHY THE HELL DO YOU WANT TO GET MARRIED ANYWAY?

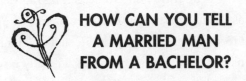

HOW CAN YOU TELL A MARRIED MAN FROM A BACHELOR?

The bachelor comes home, looks in the fridge, then goes to bed. The married man comes home, looks in the bed, then goes to the fridge.

Cold feet. It's natural. You're taking one of the biggest steps in your life, and it's perfectly normal to have second thoughts about getting married. Your friends have begun to make fun of you, saying things like

- "God, I can't believe that you are getting married."
- "Man, how does it feel to know that you're not gonna get any from anyone else again?"
- "No way, not me, no sir, I like playing the field."
- "I can't believe that you're not going to hang with us anymore."

You may think about what these jokers have said and wonder if you are doing the right thing. You think, "Why the hell am I doing this? Do I really want to spend the rest of my life with her?"

Remember all those nights out cruising the strip and at the local singles bar looking to score, checking out the chicks, and being rejected? Remember how hard it was to get psyched up to ask a girl out? Remember all those nights you went home by yourself? Was it that much fun? Yeah, you had some good times with your buddies, but is it worth giving her up for those good times? And all your pals, no matter how close they are, will not keep you warm at night.

You may feel like you are too young to be getting married. Marriage is for old people. Well, you're not seventeen anymore. You are older. Do you want to spend the rest of your life alone? Think about your old Uncle Stanley, the confirmed bachelor. The guy is so hard up you can see him coming a mile away. He's sixty years old, not gay, and is so stuffy and opinionated he needs to "get some" to loosen up a little. Do you want to wind up like him?

You think long and hard about the questions above and the answer is a resounding yes! *Yes!* She means everything to me. *Yes!* I want to spend the rest of my life with her. *Yes!* I do want to get married. (If your answer was no, you better re-evaluate your current situation, buddy.)

 "An average contemporary United States couple can still expect almost thirty years of married life together, even with recent high rates of divorce."
—from G. Robina Quale, *A History of Marriage Systems*

Just because you are getting married doesn't mean you won't see your friends anymore. It just means you can't go out cruising babes. Why would you want to anyway? You are marrying the greatest girl in the world! It doesn't mean that you can't look at a pretty girl anymore. You aren't dead, you know. You can look, but you just can't touch. (Like you really could have scored even if you could touch.)

So suck it up. Stop feeling sorry for yourself and questioning the future; it's not that bad. Marriage isn't the end of your life—it's the beginning of a wonderful relationship between two people who love each other.

YOUR FIANCÉE

Today's brides are older, well traveled, and more experienced, and many have careers. But when it comes to planning a wedding they all become little girls again.

Your wedding planning and marriage are supposed to rely on teamwork, right? You and your fiancée acting as one? Well, guess what? In this game of wedding planning, you're not the quarterback . . . you're the kicker and, therefore, will only be called in a few times during the wedding-planning game. Traditionally, the wedding planning has been all mother and daughter. In other words, coach and quarterback. They obviously have a special relationship that no kicker can ever compete with, so don't try. Don't expect to be the quarterback, in the limelight, calling the plays. That's your fiancée's job. Maybe you'll get lucky and kick the game winner. Not likely, though. Her mother, the coach, typically calls the plays but may allow your fiancée, the quarterback, to call her own or appear to call her own, every once in a while. Think back to your days playing peewee sports. I'll bet you can remember some of your coaches' peculiarities and their motivational speeches. Whether we like it or not, most coaches have a profound impact on our outlook of things. They tend to dictate our thinking and how we play the game. "Coaches'" pre-game pep talks are amazing at motivating the "players" to think and act their way. Look at the bright side: At least you're *on* the team, right?

I want to start out by telling you that this is **not your wedding.**

You have not dreamed of this day since you were a kid. This is your fiancée's day. Okay, I know what you're thinking: "What's this guy talking about, it's my wedding too." Yes, you're right, but only partly right. Have you been dreaming of "Princess Charming" all your life? Did you have talks with your dad about the lovely tuxedo you are going to wear on your wedding day? Did you just happen to look at engagement rings with your friends when you were in high school? Did you drool over your parents' wedding pictures? Did you sit at relatives' weddings taking notes and critiquing everything from center-pieces to the mothers' dresses? No, No, No, No, and No. And I'm sure you haven't dreamed about being prince for a day either!

With that said, I want you to know that the wedding is for her, not for you. This is what every little girl dreams about. It's her big day in the spotlight to look beautiful for her new husband, her family, and her friends. She gets to play Cinderella at the fancy ball, whisked back and forth in her chariot with her handmaidens at her side. Then she rides off into the sunset with her Prince Charming and they live happily ever after. Sounds like a fairy tale? Well, they really believe that kind of crap. Go ahead, let her live in her fantasy world for a day . . . even during the wedding-planning year; it won't kill you. Let other people like the rude caterer burst her bubble, but you remain her knight in shining armor. It's our job to make them feel like they are getting the whole shebang. Remember these things. They will haunt you throughout this book.

Guys, after you have digested this book, pass it on to your fiancée. This book will be good medicine for her. She should view the wedding from your perspective. What's fair is fair. There are only so many bridal magazines and pictures of dresses you can handle . . . it's her turn now!

PMS AND PMS² . . . WHAT THE HECK IS WRONG WITH HER?

As you can now tell, I'm not tippy-toeing around anything! PMS stands for two things. The first is what you expect and have come to know and love each month. I don't have to describe any of the rantings and ravings of "her monthly visitor." But take that and compound it with planning a wedding and the thought of starting a new life with someone, and what you get is Premarital Stress, or PMS². PMS² can be your worst nightmare. The emotional swings she usually experiences during her "normal" cycle will be enhanced tenfold during your engagement. Bear with them and consider the alternative: Are you ready to deal with Junior? PMS, whether one or two, is a fact of life; it happens, expect it, and don't let it affect your relationship with your fiancée. Watch it: PMS² can sneak up on you, then . . . WHAM. It will pass, but stay alert. PMS² is like a fourth-down fake punt; it happens when you least expect it.

> "A Babylonian priestess was forbidden to bear children herself. She had to provide her husband with a concubine (either a free woman or a slave) to bear them, and [the priestess] raised them for her own household."
>
> —from G. Robina Quale, *A History of Marriage Systems*

Whatever you do, don't ever let little arguments and disagreements revert to personal attacks against each other. The minute you go on the offensive, calling her names and questioning her rationality and sanity, you are opening yourself up for major problems. Your fiancée is not the enemy, as illogical as she may seem. Always talk about your differences and work them out together. Be patient, and never let your emotions get out of hand. We're guys! We're in control, right?

BROWNIE-POINT SYSTEM

Throughout the book you will see various references to brownie points. Brownie points are nothing more than credit for doing something nice, saying the right thing, or acting like the Prince Charming that your fiancée is marrying. Brownie points can keep you in good graces with your fiancée, her family, and even your family. They may even provide your fiancée with untold bragging rights among her girlfriends. Shoot for brownie points at all times. Make up your own as you go along. With a little extra effort you can keep your fiancée very happy throughout the entire wedding-planning process and through your new life together. Remember, when she is happy, you are happy too (sex innuendo).

PERFECTION

Perfection. Forget it! It doesn't exist. Humans are not supposed to be perfect. Don't expect your wedding to be perfect either. This doesn't mean you can't have a wonderful wedding; it means that if some little thing goes wrong, you and your fiancée don't want to strangle each other and the effeminate flower guy. Most of your guests will never even notice these little "problems" anyway. Perfection is only in the eye of the beholder. If you set yourself up expecting a "perfect" wedding, you are setting yourself up for failure. Relax and have fun, you *will* have a great wedding!

Actually, any little "problem" or "mishap" that occurs during your wedding can later be an excellent source of entertainment.

These "bloopers" can help you remember certain parts of the ceremony for their comedic value. You and your wife may not think these "mishaps" are very funny during the wedding, but give it a few months, and you'll both be laughing!

The day before our wedding the priest celebrating our wedding mass canceled to attend some "urgent" out-of-town prayer conference. I guess saving souls and partying with the other priests was more important than honoring the commitment that he made to us ten months before. Nice of him to tell us during the rehearsal. What did we do? Panic was not an option. Another priest filled in, and he was great. Everyone felt at ease and commented on what a beautiful ceremony we had.

MORAL OF THE STORY:
Relax and enjoy yourself. There are very few things in life that should spoil your wedding. It's not worth raising your blood pressure and ruining your wedding.

Don't panic if:
- you pop a button on your jacket
- your zipper won't close
- you get a white limo instead of a black one
- the best man drops the ring
- the flower girl cries
- one of your groomsmen trips walking down the aisle and falls flat on his face
- the maid of honor is so nervous, she faints

ASSUMPTIONS

You know the old saying "To assume is to make an ass out of you and me." Well, here goes. The general assumption throughout this book is that most of you guys will be having your first "traditional" or "quasi-traditional" wedding, with more than a handful of people attending. For the sake of argument, guys are responsible for "guy things" and girls are responsible for "girl things." The finances will be divvied up along somewhat "traditional" lines, with the bride's family bearing the majority of the financial burden. I will provide you with a list of your "traditional" responsibilities, including your money obligations. Now that I've told you all that, forget it, because this is your wedding and there are no rules. Your wedding is what you make of it.

On their honeymoon the husband, a real big guy, lineman type, asks his wife to try on his pants and walk around with them on. She looks at him like he's crazy. She is half his size. He insists. So she does. The pants wrap around her waist two times. "I can't wear your pants!" she shouts. Exerting his manliness, he bellows, "You're damn right you can't wear my pants, and don't forget it! I'm the one who wears the pants in this family!"

Not to be outdone, the bride takes off her panties and hands them to her husband. "Try these on," she says. "I can't get into these," he grumbles. Triumphantly she states, "That's right, and that's the way it's going to be until you change your attitude, mister!"

CHAPTER 2

THE PROPOSAL

THE THREE RINGS
OF MARRIAGE:

Engagement Ring
Wedding Ring
Suffering

TO POP THE QUESTION OR NOT TO POP THE QUESTION? THAT IS THE QUESTION.

It's probably too late. You jumped the gun and got engaged without reading this book. That's okay. This section is for those smart, prepared guys who did their research ahead of time and bought my book. If you're already engaged, you may want to skip to Chapter 3.

THE ENGAGEMENT RING

You have seen all the Cindy Crawford commercials about buying your fiancée rings and jewelry. Now, instead of paying attention to Cindy, it's time to pay attention to the jewelry. The jewelry industry has tried to convince guys to spend two months', three months' worth of salary, or more, on an engagement ring. Forget it. It doesn't mean anything. It's a marketing ploy by the jewelry industry to get you to spend as much money on an engagement ring as possible. The key to remember is that your fiancée will be wearing this ring on her finger, hopefully forever. Girls are funny about engagement rings. Other girls will judge you, your livelihood, and to some extent your manliness, and will also judge their husband's or fiancé's manly prowess, by this stupid ring. It can make you feel like they are comparing crotch sizes! (Didn't mean to put the pressure on you.) You may say, "My sweetie is not that pretentious. In fact, she's very modest." Sure she is, buddy! Just watch her after she gets her ring.

She may even say, "I'm not that shallow. How could you think that? I'm hurt! It's not the ring that means anything to me, it's your love." Watch her. It's a constant hand-grabbing, oohing and aahing fest with her girlfriends. They will continue to grab each other's hands well after you're married to view this piece of compressed carbon. Don't get me wrong: I'm not telling you to go out and mortgage your life away for a ring, or to succumb to ridiculous pressure from the jewelry industry, your fiancée, or her friends. But I am saying that it is important to know what you are doing when you purchase a ring. There aren't too many guys who know the difference between a marquise- and a brilliant-shaped stone. But go and ask any girl whether married, engaged, or hopelessly single, and all of them can explain the difference. Get her the ring she wants, not what you like. She has to wear it on her finger. Cubic zirconias don't count! Forget the TV home-shopping clubs. A nice ring is major, major brownie points for years to come!

Maybe you have talked about getting engaged and it is no secret. If that's the case, it makes buying the engagement ring easy. Take her to a jewelry store and find out what she likes. Although diamonds are by far the most popular stone of choice for an engagement ring, other stones may also be selected. Have her try on different shapes and sizes. You will probably sweat through this whole process and it will feel awkward; that's natural, but do it if you can. Also, remember that she doesn't have to be present when you actually purchase the ring. It can still be a surprise. I'll talk about actually proposing to her later.

If she has no idea that you are thinking about proposing to her and you want to surprise her with a ring, pay attention to her. Find out the type of jewelry she likes. Does she wear gold or silver? Does she like gaudy or simple jewelry? What size ring does she wear? If she is like most other girls, anxiously anticipating that she will be getting married some day in the near future, she will show you, and even tell you, the type of ring that she likes. Watch her with her girlfriends. You never noticed before or paid much attention to girlie coffee-klatching talk, but ladies discuss these things. After she's through looking at a friend's ring she will comment, "I hate heart-shaped stones, they look so tacky," or "Oh, her ring was soooo beautiful! Her fiancé did a great job." This last statement is a good way to judge her taste. But don't ever get her the same ring as someone she knows. Major faux pas.

Now that you've figured out the type of ring she wants, it's up to you to come through with the perfect engagement ring that she will wear forever. The three keys to finding the perfect engagement ring are:

- Shop
- Shop
- Shop

All right, I know you hate to shop—I do too. But I'm going to show you an easy way to do it. I have even provided you with an engagement-ring-shopping form in Chapter 6 at the back of the book, to make it simple. Just fill in the blanks. This formula for shopping can later be applied to your other required purchases. Trust me: Once you get this shopping thing down, it will make your life much easier.

FORMULA FOR SHOPPING

1. **Investigate**
2. **Establish Common Criteria**
3. **Compare**

INVESTIGATE

- Visit local jewelers. Take her with you if it's not a surprise.
- Talk to her mother, sisters, and friends to get ideas (always make sure these people can keep a secret).

- Talk to your sisters and mother for ideas . . . whatever you do, don't ask any of your buddies, unless they are already married. Otherwise, you are just setting yourself up for potential ridicule.
- Determine the shape of the diamond that your honey prefers.
- Read any literature about engagement rings you can find.

ESTABLISH COMMON CRITERIA

Certified diamonds and the five C's

To effectively shop for a diamond you need to establish common criteria. You can purchase your diamond at the local mall, in a small shop, and through so-called wholesalers. But how do you know that the diamond you are buying is a quality stone? In your vast trek to find the perfect engagement ring, you will encounter diamond certifications and the five C's: Color, Cut, Clarity, Carat, and Cost.

CERTIFICATIONS

The Gemological Institute of America (GIA) serves the jewelry industry by grading or certifying diamonds—in essence, establishing common criteria so that you can shop. They don't buy, sell, or appraise jewelry. They describe only the facts of a particular diamond: the weight, proportions, finish, color grade, and clarity grade. (They won't, however, provide the fifth C, cost. That's the retailer's job.) This description of the "facts" is called a GIA certification. The GIA will provide the retailer with an actual certificate stating the "facts" of the diamond, and the certificate should be provided to you at the time of purchase.

Not all diamonds are certified, since there are extra costs involved, but without a certification you are at the mercy of the jewelry retailer to accurately and ethically present the five C's to you. Yeah, right! Anyone can call themselves a jeweler or a gemologist.

Artie, the diamond broker with the pinkie rings, shirt unbuttoned to his navel, and fifteen gold chains around his neck, does not have your best interests at heart. He wants to make a buck and will tell you almost anything to close the sale. Without the certification, you don't stand a chance of getting accurate information. What you get is Artie's appraisal of the diamond. Make sure you get the GIA certificate.

THE FIVE C'S

Color

Diamonds come in many different colors, such as blue, brown, red, pink, orange, and black. But for the sake of argument, we will concern ourselves only with colorless stones or stones with a yellow-ish tint. A totally colorless diamond is referred to as "perfect" and allows light to pass through and reflect a beautiful rainbow prism. The closer the diamond is to being perfect, the greater its value. Just a small step in quality from near colorless to colorless can cause the price to skyrocket. The more "color" a stone has, the yellower it is and the less it is worth relative to size. (A smaller yellowed stone is worth less than a larger yellowed stone with similar specifications.)

The GIA has developed a scale to rate the coloring of a diamond. The GIA color scale starts with grade D and runs through grade U. The stones get progressively yellower the further down the alphabet you go. Grades D–I appear colorless. Grades J–Q are increasingly yellow. In grades R–U, the stone appears yellow.

Cut

The cut of the stone refers to its proportions and is very impor-tant to its overall appearance. A poorly cut diamond will not reflect light correctly and will make the stone appear dull. One of the best types of cuts is the "ideal cut." The ideal cut provides the best pro-portioning of the stone and allows a better flow of light through it.

Not all stones can have an ideal cut. Make sure your jeweler shows you the difference between ideal-cut stones and other stones.

Sometimes people confuse the cut with the shape of the diamond. Diamonds are "cut" into shapes such as oval, pear, heart, emerald, marquise, round, and so on.

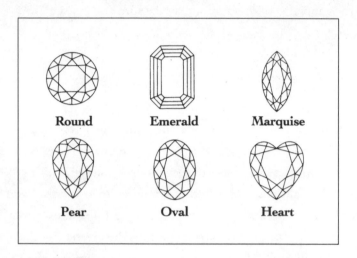

Clarity

Clarity refers to the internal and external flaws of the diamond. The clarity is ranked according to the flaws, or inclusions, in the stone. Flaws and inclusions can be cracks (feathers) or black spots. Be careful: Make sure that these feather cracks are not filled, since Artie may be trying to pass something off on you. The GIA will not certify filled diamonds.

The GIA has developed a scale to rate the clarity of a diamond. The grading scale runs from FL, flawless, to I3, or severely flawed. The lower you go on the list the more flawed the stone, which lowers its value.

Carat

Karat, carat, or carrot? The K refers to the purity of gold, which you won't have to worry about until later. "Carat" refers to the

**No internal or external flaws visible with the
gem microscope**

FL	flawless
IF	internally flawless
VVS1	very very slightly included (flawed)

Flaws difficult to view under the gem microscope

VVS2	very very slightly included
VS1	very slightly included
VS2	very slightly included
SI1	slightly included
SI2	slightly included

Can see the flaws with the naked eye

I1	included
I2	included

Looks nasty

I3	severely included

weight of the stone, and "carrot" refers to the orange thing you eat. Diamonds are usually described in terms of carats and points. One carat equals one hundred points. Prices are quoted in dollars per points. For your fiancée's sake, the larger the better, and she probably only likes talking in whole numbers . . . one carat, two carats, three carats, four. Forget the fractions, like $1/16$ carat. Slivers don't count. Color, cut, and clarity determine the per-carat dollar value. This means that a large stone is not necessarily more expensive than a much smaller stone that has better color, cut, and clarity. For similar stones, prices increase exponentially as the stones get larger. A two-carat stone with the same characteristics as a one-carat stone is not double the price; it is much, much more expensive!

Cost

Probably the most important of the five C's. Determine your budget. How much can you afford? Does your little pookie really want a nice, expensive ring? You may wind up putting that new car you wanted on her finger.

SETTINGS

The setting of the stone is also important. The setting refers to the way that the diamond will be placed on an engagement-ring band. (Please note that this band is different from the wedding band. The wedding band is a totally separate ring that she will wear after you are married, not before.) Typically, the engagement-ring band is made of gold or platinum. Platinum is preferred since it is much stronger than gold, but it is also more expensive than gold. Silver is not often used. The stone is usually set on the engagement-ring band with platinum prongs locking the stone in place. There are literally endless setting possibilities. You can add stones or have the setting produced to accommodate her wedding band, since some wedding bands and engagement rings are predesigned to fit together with interlocking patterns. The choice is hers. Many jewelers have the ability to custom design a setting. Have the jeweler show you some of the things that he can do. Make sure that you know her ring size. It's easier to have it sized right in the beginning than to have it cut and resized to fit her finger later.

COMPARE

After you have taken some time to determine the five C's, grab your trusty telephone, engagement-ring shopping form from Chapter 6 at the back of the book, and pencil. You are ready to begin your comparison shopping. Make sure you have highlighted the exact specifications that you're looking for in the five C's on your form. Now, take out your yellow pages and start at the top. Since you have already investigated, have been to a few stores shopping around, and have established your common criteria and know the exact type of stone you are looking for, you can compare prices with all the different retailers. Remember, no two stones will be exactly alike. Many retailers may come close to your perfect stone but not match it exactly. That's okay. After you select the stone that sounds best, make sure you visit the store to see it in person. If this isn't a surprise for your fiancée, bring her along and make sure she loves it. It's very important to get a receipt and, if the stone is certified, a GIA certificate. (Remember, not all stones are certified.)

Besides the education I just provided you, there's always more for you to know. Shop, shop, shop.

If you are surprising your girlfriend with the ring, some jewelers will allow you to purchase the ring "on approval." This means that if she hates the ring, you can exchange it for another.

After you purchase the engagement ring, check with your insurance provider about having the ring insured. You just spent a big chunk of change—make sure it's covered. You will probably have to add a rider to your existing policy.

PROPOSING

You have the ring and you're ready to pop the question. Even if she knows that you bought the ring, she doesn't have to know when or how you are going to give it to her. Surprises can be fun, but they can also be dangerous. Be careful: In most cases, you will be in unfamiliar waters.

You have heard about the guy getting engaged at halftime of the football game or the guy who places "Will you marry me, Jane?" on the scoreboard at the ballpark. These are great ideas and considered romantic by most guys, but, to be honest, it takes a very special woman to appreciate our sense of romanticism. Most ladies don't value it the way we do. Remember, the wedding is for her, and that means the engagement is for her as well.

Guys, remember when I told you about how girls look at each other's engagement rings and judge you by these rings? Well, the same applies to how you propose. Get in touch with your feminine side, think romantic. Romanticism means a lot of things to a lot of different people. Do what will feel right to you and, most important, will feel right to her. Do something special and memorable that both of you will enjoy. Major brownie points earned for a special proposal.

I tend to feel that an engagement is a private thing and should be encountered by the couple first and not the entire world, or the extended family. After you are engaged you will have plenty of time to tell everyone. Therefore, my engagement idea list is geared toward doing the "couple thing." I'll go through the protocol of notifying family and friends afterward.

 "When a man elopes with a girl without her parents' approval he reverts to methods of the most primitive times, marriage by capture."

—from Frank Klock, *Apes and Husbands*

HOW TO GET ENGAGED

Some ideas for popping the question:

- Spend the weekend at a bed-and-breakfast.
- Spend the weekend at the beach.

- Surprise her with dinner at a fancy restaurant. (Don't tell the waiter to sing some corny "Happy Engagement to You" song either.) Rent a limo and take her out on the town.
- Cook dinner for her with candles, a tablecloth, flowers, romantic music, and all that mushy stuff.
- Go on a picnic.

Gill cooked a wonderful gourmet dinner for his soon-to-be fiancée, complete with champagne and chocolate-covered strawberries. He presented her with a bouquet of a dozen red roses, and in the middle was a jewelry box in the shape of a red rose that contained the engagement ring . . . I had to tell you about it; my wife thought it was a cute story.

Don't do it:

- Don't put her ring in her champagne; she might drink it. And don't bury it in her chocolate mousse either.
- No billboard advertisements.
- Forget the skywriter.
- Don't give her the ring in the bathroom, kitchen, or garage. (You think I'm kidding, but my brother-in-law got engaged in his garage.)

Yes, you have to get down on one knee and *ask* her to marry you. It's very important. Believe me, her mother and friends will ask her if you got down on your knee. Yeah, yeah, I know you're thinking it's stupid, but it'll make her happy. Major brownie points if you do. It's that whole Prince Charming rigmarole.

Don't let her ask you either. Here's a typical female-initiated wedding proposal:

"Do you want to get married?" she says

"Well, *uhh,* do you?" he asks.

"You know I do," she whines back.

"*Uhh,* I guess so," he says halfheartedly.

That's not a proposal. It's a "Do you want to go and get a pizza and beer?" question. Yes, it serves the purpose, but is that how you want to remember your engagement? You should ask her, on bended knee, "Will you marry me?" Stick her name in there too; it makes the proposal even more personal.

Carl asked his girlfriend to marry him while they were flying from Miami to New York. He borrowed the flight attendant's microphone and went to town. He basically proposed to the whole plane. She accepted, but their marriage only lasted six months.

MORAL OF THE STORY:
Maybe the proposal set the tone for their marriage?

You may be wondering about asking her father for her hand in marriage. I believe that asking her father is very admirable, and shows concern for tradition and for her family. But you better ask her first and make sure that she accepts the ring. There is nothing more embarrassing than putting her on the spot in front of her family and having her laugh at you.

Okay, it's done. You're engaged. You were smart and didn't tell too many people beforehand, just in case she said no. Now you must begin the tedious, all-day affair of telling people the big news. Happy!

Make sure you "have a smile in your voice." Priority number one: Call her parents and any stepparents. (You may ask her father for her hand: "I've asked your daughter to marry me. I hope we have your blessing." More brownie points earned.) Next, call your parents; then let the chips fall where they may. Don't mix up the order . . . make sure her parents are the first ones to know.

Tom and Beth went on a cruise to celebrate two years of dating. Over the past year they had talked about getting engaged but never had a serious conversation about it. Good ole Tom took it upon himself to buy an engagement ring for her. He told both families and all their friends that he was surprising her with the ring on the cruise. He asked them all to be at the dock when the ship returned. Well, guess what? Lovely Beth said no! They returned from the cruise and were greeted by a cheering mob of family and friends, who congratulated them, kissed and hugged them. Big-mouth Tom had to tell everyone she said no. Needless to say, it was an embarrassing situation.

MORAL OF THE STORY:
Don't blab about the engagement until you're actually engaged.

PARENTS' FIRST MEETING

If both sets of parents have not yet met, tradition dictates that the groom's family make the gesture. This can mean having your mom call her mother and invite them over for coffee or you planning a nice dinner out with both sets of parents. If your folks live out of the area and can't readily meet with her parents, don't force the issue. It may be easier to keep the parents apart until the rehearsal dinner. That way too many conflicting personalities are not intimately involved in the planning. This is a very touchy situation. I know that many of you will want to have both sets of parents actively involved, and they should be. But if you have any hesitation or are worried about personality clashes, opt to hold off on introductions until the rehearsal. By then, it's probably too late for any major changes in the wedding and the parents are usually more concerned with being polite to the future in-laws instead of last-minute alterations anyway. As fair as the parents think they will be, each has their own agenda at heart. (See "Your Parents, In-laws, and Other Relatives" in Chapter 3.)

"Until the nineteenth century a common custom in parts of Great Russia was for a father to marry off his son at a tender age to a young woman, and then take the woman as his own concubine until the son grew up. When the son matured, his wife had several children and was middle-aged. The son then repeated the process."

—from Frank Klock, *Apes and Husbands*

WEDDING PLANNING

**If marriage is an institution . . .
you're about to be committed for life!**

THE ENGAGEMENT

Now the fun starts. You're all engaged with no place to go. I'm going to highlight some of the key areas of planning a wedding that concern you, the groom. I'll cover most of the important wedding info that you'll need, but some of these highlights may not apply to your particular situation. Keep in mind that there is no right or wrong way to prepare for a wedding.

What I'm about to say may sound crazy, but I haven't lost my mind and, in the end, you'll thank me. Here goes . . . **don't get involved!**

Let me explain, before you get bent out of shape. Obviously, you need to take part in your own wedding—that's the whole reason for this book, and proper wedding planning can be a fun and rewarding experience. But I'm going to reiterate the resounding theme of this book: "It's *her* wedding . . . not yours." This doesn't mean that you will have no say; it means that she should have the ultimate say and you should make things as easy for her as possible. Your fiancée will go through some very trying times, as will you. Your job is to provide stability. You must remain her "Rock of Gibraltar." She will experience the full gamut of womanly emotions. She will be so overjoyed that she cries. She will be so excited, she cries. She will be so sad, she cries. She will be so mad, she cries. Expect it, because it happens to even the strongest lady . . . and to some guys too. In your supporting role, you need to be her sounding board and bitching dummy (similar to a punching dummy except you get assaulted verbally.

Sometimes, you'll think that being a punching dummy would be easier.) Let her take her frustrations out on you, because whether you like it or not, she will. Get used to it and don't get upset with her when she does. You may be tempted to "fix" things for her and solve her wedding "problems." You probably can't fix the majority of things, and she probably just wants to vent her frustrations anyway. Let her bounce her ideas off you or cry on your shoulder. Let her complain about her parents. Even let her complain about your parents. Don't yell at her. She may feel like everyone is ganging up on her. You need to be there to reaffirm her decisions and let her know she is doing a good job. Ask her if you can help.

**Wedding planning and your marriage
are supposed to be partnerships . . .
and you are the silent partner.**

THE "RIGHT OF FIRST REFUSAL"

I just made your day, fellas. I'm about to show you a way to stay active and participate in the wedding planning without getting in her way or boring yourself to death with minutiae. It's called the "Right of First Refusal."

RULES OF THE GAME:

1. It's your fiancée's obligation to pick the products and services that she wants. You don't get in her way or make comments or criticisms to her during the selection process. She has total freedom to plan things her way.

2. Once she has made a decision regarding a specific product or service, she is required to run her idea by you for approval. If, and only if, you absolutely hate her idea, it's then her responsibility to go back and reselect. When you refuse something, it's your obligation to explain to your fiancée why you did not like her idea and, in turn, offer her alternatives. After she reselects, the process is repeated and you have the right to refuse again. Guys, keep in mind that when it's your turn to tackle a specific product or service, she has the same "Right of First Refusal" you had.

The "Right of First Refusal" gives you the ability to stay involved in your wedding planning without aggravating your fiancée. If you discuss this method of wedding planning with her before you both get deeply involved in the process, you will have much better success planning your wedding.

"Right of First Refusal" does not mean you play the "Gestapo Dictator from Hell," who rules with an iron fist over his fiefdom. It means that you will play an active part in the planning and are now "involved," and not just a toy soldier. You should only refuse those things that are utterly disgusting to you. Things that you moderately hate should be accepted. Remember, your fiancée took a long time and devoted a lot of effort to arrive at some of her decisions. If and when you refuse something you must talk to her about it. Your dearly beloved could take your refusal personally and could even interpret it to mean: "Why are you even marrying me if I have no taste?" Explain to her why you don't like her decision, since she is the one who will have to go back and reselect. (Guys, "because I said so" is not a reason to reselect.) Also, if you refuse too much, she is going to throw it back in your face and tell you to do it. Lord knows, you don't want to have to select the flowers, her tiara, or her veil. If you invoke your "Right of First Refusal," it's your responsibility to explain why you don't like the idea and, in turn, provide your fiancée with alternative ideas. So guys, walk that fine line and it can be easy planning.

Anticipate having fights, but don't let the fight progress to personal attacks against each other. Work things out! Compromise.

I recommend showing this section to your fiancée and letting her read it so that you don't screw up the explanation of "Right of First Refusal" and make bigger problems for yourself. Get her to agree to it before you start planning. If she doesn't understand your methods and reasoning, or the "Right of First Refusal," she may think you don't care. Present the "Right of First Refusal" pledge in Chapter 6 to your fiancée and make sure she understands it. After she has read it, make sure you both sign the bottom. Keep it with your "playbook" (the "playbook" is covered later in this chapter) and refer to it whenever necessary.

EXEMPTIONS FROM THE "RIGHT OF FIRST REFUSAL"

She doesn't need your approval for:

- Her dress
- Her personal accessories
- The bridesmaids' dresses

DIVIDING UP RESPONSIBILITIES

Most of the wedding planning will revolve around her. She will need to make the vast majority of decisions. Stereotypical gender lines tend to dictate who does what. Each of the categories to follow will be highlighted with **Bride, Groom,** or **Both of You.** Stay true to your gender, and the process will be painless. When you venture where nature did not intend for man to be, there can be problems.

CONTRACTS

BOTH OF YOU

The old adage "Get it in writing" applies to your wedding. Many of the goods and services you'll be purchasing will have to be paid for in advance, in full. This isn't to protect you, it's to protect the vendor. Make sure that you get everything in writing. Don't settle for the vendor's word. If they won't put it in writing, don't give them the money they want in advance. It's that simple. Most will require cash or a check (no credit cards). If you have a problem the day of the wedding, good luck trying to get your money back! Protect yourself, and make sure you get exactly what you are paying for. Put it in writing.

Carla and Randy walked into their reception, and everything was perfect except that there was no cake! The baker simply forgot. The caterer had the good sense to go to a local grocery store and purchase several sheet cakes, so that the couple had a cake to cut and serve to the guests.

MORAL OF THE STORY:
No contract was signed, so the couple had no recourse. Get everything in writing.

Contract tips:

- Don't let your emotions interfere with your negotiations.
- Use your fax machine at home or work to get quotes in writing.
- Get any contractual changes in writing.

- Always negotiate the lowest possible deposit.
- Ask for references.
- Make sure your deposits can be refunded and that there are no large cancellation fees hidden in the contract.
- Always use credit cards whenever possible (this makes it easier to get your money back).
- Read the fine print.
- Always ask for what you want. If you don't ask, you don't get!

Elements that should be included in the contracts:

- The actual day, date, and time of the wedding
- The date the contract is signed
- A detailed list of all merchandise ordered and a list of services that are provided by the vendor
- The list should include: number of hours for services, time to report, how many breaks will be taken, what type of clothing the vendors will be wearing, and vendor points of contact with phone numbers
- A detailed payment schedule and the deposit amounts required
- The deadline for last-minute changes and for the final guest count
- A detailed procedure for how contract changes will be handled
- The refund and cancellation policy
- How much overtime will cost, if necessary

VENDOR GUILT AND PRICE-QUOTE HELL

Typically, these same vendors that must have payment in advance are famous for giving you a major guilt complex. They'll tell you that to make your wedding perfect you must choose the superpremium package for $50,000, when the standard package for $5,000 will work for you. They will try to guilt you into something you don't want or need. Be careful—the good ones will do it without you realizing it.

You have established common criteria (see Chapter 2) and, armed with your trusty yellow pages, you begin calling around to get the best possible quotes. Mr. Vendor says that he can't possibly give you a quote over the phone since he customizes each wedding. (Yeah, right!) What this means is that he is afraid to give you a price since he thinks it will scare you off, or that you are the nasty evil competitors trying to steal his prices. If he doesn't want to play ball, call another vendor.

GOOD COP, BAD COP

You have all seen the detective movies where two cops interrogate the criminal to get him to confess to a crime or get him to give them the info they need to make the big bust. One guy is the "good" cop while the other is the "bad" cop. The "good" cop pretends to be the criminal's friend. He talks to him, builds his trust, then, *wham,* in rushes the screaming "bad" cop and throws the criminal against the wall. The "good" cop rushes over to save the day and "protects" the convict from his partner. The "bad" cop leaves the room and the "good" cop tells the slime that his partner is an asshole and that he won't be able to protect him much longer. He makes a deal with the crook. If the criminal will tell him what he needs to know, he will make sure the "bad" cop won't get him and he'll be let go.

Obviously, you're not going to slam the vendors against the wall even though, at times, it may feel like you're getting robbed. Play the game. Whoever makes the first contact with a vendor is the "good" cop (this can be your fiancée, you, or both of you). Before finalizing a contract tell the vendor that you have to check with the "bad cop" (this could be you, your fiancée, her mother, or her father). You then go back to the vendor and make your demands. Your fiancée says, "Mr. Vendor, I am sorry but my father is paying for the wedding and he says $1,000 is too much and he can't afford it. He said he can only pay $750 and that ABC Company would do it for $750 and he told me I had to use them." You can even have her father show up and play the "bad cop" role. Watch the vendor squirm and do the deal for $750!

Most of the time, this technique works. However, there are times when the vendor won't budge and you will have to pay up or shut up. A different play on the good cop, bad cop game is to pit one vendor against another. Decide on the vendor you want. Go to a competitor and get a quote in writing that is lower than your pre-ferred vendor. Show it to him and ask him to match it. There is a good chance that they will. *Everything is negotiable!!*

THE BETTER BUSINESS BUREAU AND REFERENCES

I'm not a big fan of the Better Business Bureau (BBB). You've heard people say, "Check with the BBB to make sure you are dealing with a reputable company." The BBB is an organization that is sup-ported by businesses. They charge businesses to become members, give them a plaque to put in their offices, then call them if a customer has a complaint. Since they are supported by businesses, it makes sense that they don't want to bite the hand that feeds them. The BBB keeps files on all member and nonmember companies. If a consumer calls the BBB and asks about a certain company, the BBB will advise the consumer if the business has any unresolved complaints. Here's the catch: The BBB is only an intermediary, a middleman. They simply ask the company to take action. It is totally up to the company to resolve the problem. The BBB has absolutely no leverage or influence over the company. When the company feels they have settled the matter to their satisfaction, the BBB case may be closed. If the customer got shortchanged, tough luck. Does it reflect as a negative mark against the company? Sometimes, but not always. The BBB is a good starting point for referencing companies, but I wouldn't rely solely on the recommendation of the BBB.

A better approach is to check with family and friends, and ask for their recommendations. Which companies have they had success with? Take their recommendations and call the vendors. Always ask the vendor for a list of no less than three references, and make sure you call the references. Obviously, the company won't give you bad references, but you will be able to gauge by the tone of these references how successful the vendor was at making their customers happy. If the references don't shine and say that the vendor was the best thing since sliced bread, steer clear of that vendor.

"Among the Cyrenaica Bedouin, the husband's
father was traditionally believed to see the
marriage of a son as signaling the onset of
age and weakness."

—from G. Robina Quale, *A History of Marriage Systems*

YOUR PARENTS, IN-LAWS, AND OTHER RELATIVES

BOTH OF YOU

Every parent reacts to the impending nuptials in a different way. Your mother may be completely overbearing and domineering and want everything her way. Her father may be cheap and criticize her every wish.

You *will* piss someone off!! No matter what you do or how conscientious you are, you *will* upset someone about something. Don't waste your time dwelling on the issue and trying to think of every possible way to make everyone happy. There is no way to do it. Make sure you and, most importantly, your future wife are happy. If, and when, someone is upset with you about something trivial, blow it off. (I said *blow it off,* not *tell them off.* Make note of this distinction.) It's not worth the stress. Big deal, so you sat Great-Aunt Matilda with Cousin Myron, and she hates him. You didn't know that, and if she is going to be mad because of it and not talk to you, forget her. This isn't her wedding and you already have enough stress in your life. She probably gave you that unopened hand-crank can opener that she received in 1946 as a wedding gift anyway.

With both sets of parents you have to be much more diplomatic, of course. Run interference with the families and keep the bride as happy as possible. Just pick and roll. This is your very first chance dealing with family politics. How you react to different wedding stresses will mean mucho brownie points or minus brownie points with your sweetie and her family. It's okay to express your opinions, but whatever you do, don't argue with her parents. You should always be on your best behavior, whether dealing with Great-Aunt Matilda or Grandpa Joe. Being an ass won't get you anywhere, except maybe starting married life with her family hating your guts.

If you have successfully alienated her parents due to your incredible tact and manners, it's up to you to make amends. I don't care if her father started it, you have to live with his daughter for the rest of your life. Suck it up, and do what you have to do to keep the peace. What, are you going to have everyone pissed off at you on your wedding day? Deal with it. You're a big boy now—you're getting married.

Don't ever mention to or argue with her parents about the following:

- Politics
- How bitchy their daughter has been since she started planning the wedding
- Abortion
- Gays in the military and other controversial topics
- Sex (her dad doesn't want to hear anything about his daughter being able to tie a cherry stem into a knot with her tongue)

"Among the Chukchee of Siberia . . . the groom's parents could return the bride up to eighteen months after the marriage, even if the groom wanted to keep her."

—from G. Robina Quale, *A History of Marriage Systems*

TRADITIONS AND SUPERSTITIONS
BOTH OF YOU

"Because it's tradition." You will hear this phrase over and over. Try as you might, you won't have a clue as to what everyone is talking about. Aunt Bertha will insist that you serve dried corn kernels on the table and that without them you'll break tradition and ruin your wedding. What? Whose tradition? Ask her to explain this tradition, and why it's done, and she will say that it has always been done that way, without a clue as to why. She may give some half-baked reason like, "In the hills of Liechtenstein, farmers rubbed corn kernels on the noses of their horses to make them plow better. Which means that you must have corn kernels on the table to ensure a happy wedding and prosperous life or suffer the curse of the mad horse."

Ridiculous. It makes no sense at all, but for some strange reason it does to her. But it's not her wedding, right? Traditions are often followed blindly without a clue as to why. Every wedding is unique. Many have the same, or similar, elements or themes, but the intricacies of each are different. Traditions, superstitions, and perfection go hand in hand. They don't mean a damn thing unless they have meaning for you and your fiancée. You are free to follow any traditions that you like, or you are welcome to establish your own traditions.

 "[In early India] a woman could not talk with her husband outside their sleeping quarters until her mother-in-law had died."
—from G. Robina Quale, *A History of Marriage Systems*

ORGANIZATION AND THE "PLAYBOOK"
GROOM

It's a good idea to keep a folder or "playbook" of all the information that you'll acquire on your matrimonial planning journey. Keep all important documents and contracts in this folder. There should be a detailed "To Do" list, as well as a detailed itinerary of the rehearsal dinner, wedding, reception, honeymoon, and tips and fees that you must pay. The folder should also contain a list of all vendors and points of contact with their addresses and work and home telephone numbers. Some vendors won't give out their home telephone number, but if you can get it, it could be extremely valuable on your wedding day should you have a last-minute problem that needs to be fixed. I tend to be a very cluttered person, but I have found that even if I just shove the paperwork into one central folder, it's much easier than having to find documents, or worse, trying to re-create documents. Not only will the "playbook" keep you organized, it will also provide you with a record of the wedding preparations that your wife can keep with the wedding album and refer to in later years. "See, kids, when Grampa got married in 1999, the wedding only cost $30,000. Can you believe it? Those were the good old days!"

Try to keep the "playbook" as neat as possible, since your best man and "point man" will be working from it as well.

WEDDING CONSULTANTS, PLANNERS, AND COORDINATORS

BRIDE

I've read in some magazines and books that wedding consultants can be invaluable. They can save you money, reduce your stress level, handle family disputes, and play the "bad cop" regarding money negotiations between vendors and your family. All this may be true, but it also takes some of the fun out of planning your happy union. When you hire a wedding consultant, you are hiring another "mother" to hold your hand, walk you through the process, and basically do things their way. After everything you have been through, and will go through, do you really want a stranger telling you what to do and how things "should" be done?

It's true that wedding planners can and usually do save you money. If a wedding consultant has planned enough weddings, they can have substantial leverage with some vendors. But the money that they save you is usually not much in excess of their fees, so it becomes a wash.

A wedding coordinator is very useful for couples who both have exceedingly demanding work schedules, live far away from their wedding site, have gobs and gobs of money to blow, don't have a mother or future mother-in-law to help, or just don't want to deal with the whole thing. Planners also work best for those couples who can't make decisions and who can't successfully negotiate with their parents to have the wedding their way.

Any way you cut it, there will be stress involved with the wedding planning. Don't think you are going to rid yourself of stress by hiring a wedding coordinator. Wedding consultants can even complicate things. Now not only do you have the personalities of your fiancée, her mother, your mother, and the other relatives competing, you'll have the personality of the wedding planner clashing as well.

There is no way that a wedding won't have some little mishaps. The wedding coordinator is supposed to handle the "problems" and fix them without involving you or your bride. With proper planning, your best man, your "point man" (explained later in this chapter), and her maid of honor can tackle most problems that the wedding consultant would handle.

If you thought you didn't have a say in any of the wedding stuff before, you could really be "riding the bench" if a wedding consultant is hired.

MONEY

BRIDE (but You'll Have to Pay Through the Nose)

Whoever said "Money doesn't get in the way of love" was in left field. Money remains the root of all evil. I'm not going to pussyfoot around this one. Today, many couples bear the financial burden of their own wedding, but traditionally most of the costs were borne by the bride's family. Today's weddings can cost well in excess of $20,000. I know the wedding is for both of you, but if her family is paying for it, give them the benefit of the doubt. What are you going to do, rant and rave and threaten to call the whole thing off if you don't have a pu-pu platter for an appetizer? You think I'm kidding, but this stuff really happens. There is nothing worse than arguing about money with your fiancée before you are married. You'll have plenty of time to do that afterward.

Okay guys, we have basically established that "traditions" are for you and your fiancée to pick and choose from. Well, add traditional expenses to the list. For the sake of argument, in the pages that follow I'm going to highlight the section with a "$" when "tradition" has dictated that you (the groom) fork over the cash and pay the tab.

It would be highly advisable to get the money issues out in the open right from the get-go. Talk with her parents and with your parents and plan a budget. Find out how much her family is willing to pay and how much your family will contribute. This can be very uncomfortable, but once everyone is satisfied with who pays for what, your lives will be much easier. When the cards are laid out on the table, no one can point a finger later. Also, if you or your family commits to pay for something, make sure it's paid for in a timely manner, whether the money goes to her family or to the vendor directly.

PERCENTAGE OF BUDGET

This is only for budgetary purposes. It's perfectly fine for you to take money from one area and allocate it to another.

Your fiancée:

Reception	50%
Dress	10%
Photographs or videotaping	10%
Music	10%
Flowers	10%
Miscellaneous	6%
Invitations	4%
TOTAL BUDGET	100%

You:

Engagement ring	50%
Miscellaneous (tux, flowers, gifts, etc.)	20%
Rehearsal	12.5%
Honeymoon	12.5%
Limo	5%
TOTAL BUDGET	100%

DECIDING ON A DATE
BOTH OF YOU

The most popular month for weddings is June, and the last Saturday in June is the busiest of the year. Almost every girl wants to be a June bride. Summer is here. The weather is warm and love is in the air (*yuck*, don't throw up). That leaves you with only four weekends to have the perfect summer wedding. Not a whole heck of a lot of time. If you're planning on June, be prepared to schedule years in advance. Also, late spring and early fall tend to book up pretty fast as well. If you are looking to do a quickie wedding and are planning for one of these busy months, you could have a hard time getting exactly what you want.

One of the most common questions asked is, "What is the appropriate length of time to be engaged before getting married?" There is no right or wrong answer, although the average engagement is about fifteen months. Some do it much faster, others take a long time. If the engagement is too short you may overlook something important or your first preference may already be booked. On the other hand, if your engagement is very long you can unduly stress yourselves out and planning can become drawn out and monotonous. Pick a date that works for both of you. It can be a memorable date, such as the day you met or your parents' or grandparents' anniversary. As unromantic for your fiancée as it may seem, sometimes the date is determined by when the church or facility is available.

RELIGION, PICKING THE WEDDING SITE, AND THE CEREMONY
BOTH OF YOU

You must play by the respective rules if you want your wedding to be a religious experience. For Catholics, a priest won't marry you on the beach. If you want to have a priest celebrating your wedding mass, it must be in a church and you usually must be a parishioner. For Jews marrying outside your religion, good luck trying to find a rabbi who will marry you. It can be done, but it's a lot of work. You would think that it shouldn't be a major problem having things your way at your wedding. Well, each religion has its own quirks and dos and don'ts. Check with your place of worship for specific details. If you are having a justice of the peace perform your ceremony, don't expect them to say prayers.

Also, most religions are famous for requiring prewedding counseling. The Catholics call it Pre-Cana. You take compatibility tests and are required to attend numerous meetings with a priest, who asks you if you are having premarital sex . . . talk about Catholic guilt! All this, then they require you to attend a weekend retreat to "get to know each other" . . . of course you stay in separate rooms. You'll learn about the lovely Catholic "rhythm method" of birth control (the same birth control method that my mother-in-law had four kids using).

You may have to book the site well in advance. The length of religious counseling may dictate when you can have the wedding. For Catholics, allow six months.

Deciding on the ceremony can be tricky. If you are both Baptist and are getting married in your fiancée's hometown, you would naturally have the ceremony at her childhood church. No problem. What happens when she is Methodist and you are Muslim? Now we have a problem. You will begin to feel intense pressure from both families. There is no easy answer. You can do the "justice of the peace" thing or have concelebrants, but it's just going to be one of those no-win situations. Explain how you feel to your fiancée and work it out. Chances are, you have discussed this with her before, but if you haven't you'd better. You will have to talk to your parents and she to hers, and remember . . . it's *her* wedding!

Is it going to be formal, semiformal, or casual? At a religious house of worship, at the beach, or in your backyard? Morning, afternoon, or evening? Small, medium, large, or XL? (Would you like fries with that?)

Alternatives:

- Break up.
- Go to Vegas and visit the Elvis Drive-Thru Wedding Chapel.
- Get married on a boat in the Caribbean by yourselves.

THE LIST

BOTH OF YOU

The List. It sounds like it could be some horror novel from Stephen King. Well, it is. The List can be, by far, the most troubling aspect of planning a wedding. I have attempted to make it as easy as possible for you and your fiancée.

ELEMENTS OF THE LIST

1. You and your future wife make a list of every person that you both could possibly invite.

2. Call her parents and ask them how many people they were planning to pay for. Explain to them your ideas and the type of wedding that you and your fiancée would prefer to have. Make sure your wedding expectations and her parents' expectations are in sync. If not, you have a lot of discussing to do. The reception site may dictate the number of guests you can have, so make sure you check with someone from the reception hall as well.

3. Call both sets of parents (or stepparents) and ask them for their list of people. The money that's been budgeted by her family

is usually a lot less than all the names the List will accommodate. Add the parents' guests to the List. Incidentally, if you and your fiancée have stepparents, forget about trying to have a small wedding; it's almost impossible.

4. All these names now become your "A" list. Just like Hollywood. At the back of this book I have provided you with a sample List form and worksheet. Follow that format when preparing your List. You will need the name, address, and telephone number of each potential invitee. You will also need to decide which guests will be invited to the rehearsal dinner. This "A" list will become your "bible." You will use it to keep track of the date you sent each person their invitation, whether or not they have been invited to the rehearsal dinner, if they plan to attend the rehearsal and the reception, the gift they gave you, and the date you sent them a thank-you card.

Some wedding planners say that it's okay to invite someone to the ceremony but not invite them to the reception. This makes no sense to me at all. Why are you inviting them in the first place? I thought you wanted them to celebrate your happiness with you, which means attending the reception as well. Unless this is a shameless attempt to collect more wedding gifts, invite everyone to your reception too.

5. Begin the cut. Unfortunately, you can't invite everyone on the List, so you need to start cutting people. The people you cut don't disappear forever; they are simply moved to the "B" list. The "B" list should be for all maybes. The only way to compile an "A" and a "B" list is by trial and error.

Take a deep breath. You may reach the point where you have to tell both sets of parents, and any extended family, that they must cut their lists. You gotta do what you gotta do! Parents can be very unreasonable. Your father may insist on inviting three hundred of his closest friends from work, and her mother may want to invite the entire bridge club, when neither you nor your fiancée could care less about having his work or her bridge friends at your celebration. It has to end somewhere. It's great if that's what you want for your wedding, but typically everyone involved has their limits. If your father wants to invite these three hundred guests and there is only a budget for two hundred total guests, you have a problem. It's your responsibility to keep your family in line and her responsibility to keep her family in line. If your dad still insists on the three hundred co-workers, you may have to politely tell him he must pay for their dinner costs. What's fair is fair.

The best way to allocate wedding invitees is to allow one-third for you and your fiancée, one-third for her parents, and one-third for your parents.

6. After you have somewhat finalized your "A" list, take your "B" list and arrange the names in preference order. Anywhere from 5 to 25 percent of the people you invite will not attend the wedding. This could enable you to invite a number of people from the "B" list.

7. Make sure you send out the "A" list early to allow extra time to invite persons off the "B" list. (According to some wedding planners, it's not couth to send out invitations to a "B" list. Maybe not, but it does make economical sense from my point of view.) Timing will be very important when sending out your invitations. If you use my "A" and "B" list format, I would advise you to send the "A" list invitations out at least eight to twelve weeks before the wedding.

8. As you receive each rejection, scratch that name off the "A" list and bump the next person up from the "B" list.

9. Continually update the "A" list. Keep it clean and organized.

Things to consider when formulating the List:

- When was the last time I saw or talked to this person?
- Was I invited to his or her wedding?
- Am I inviting this person to be nice or do I *really* want them at the wedding?

- Will I ever talk to this person after the wedding?
- Will I be happy if this person is at the wedding?
- Is this person a close or a casual friend?
- Do I even know this person and do I care if they attend?

INVITATIONS
BRIDE (but You Can Try if You Like)

Unless you're in the printing business and can tell the difference between photocopies, offset printing, engraving, PMS one over one, and thermography, does it really matter? Okay, if you really want to get involved with something, maybe she'll let you handle the invitations (most guys can't screw that up too badly). However, are you going to write the mushy gobbledygook on the invitation asking your guests to "attend the loving nuptials of the beloved bride Mary Jane and her handsome and dashing stud Joe Blow"? Stay with what you know . . . put the stamps on the envelopes and the return envelopes! Don't lick the envelopes until you are sure that your List is final. If you need help on how to address the envelope, write the invitations, and properly stuff the envelope, there are literally hundreds of books and bridal magazines on the subject (visit your local bookstore or library). Usually instructions that detail how everything should be done come with the invitations. You can also have the rehearsal-dinner invitations printed to match the wedding invitations, but they can just as easily be printed on the computer and for a lot less money.

If you are inviting a buddy who is living with a girl, make sure you personalize the invitation and include her name. Don't put "and Guest" unless you're not sure which babe your friend will bring. People sometimes get bent out of shape if they are referred to as "and Guest." Make sure you send invitations to all of the wedding party, brothers and sisters and parents. Of course they know they are invited, but they would probably like to have their own keepsake.

Plan to increase your telephone budget. You went ahead and included an RSVP card with a box for "will attend" and a box for "will not attend" in the invitations that you sent. You even put a stamp on the damn thing so that it wouldn't cost them anything to send it back to you. You'd think that your close friends and relatives would be kind enough (and smart enough) to return the stupid thing to you. Well, they're not! Inevitably, you'll have to call these ignoramuses up just to find out whether or not they will attend your wedding. Sheesh!

Don't forget to order enough invitations to cover your "B" list.

FLOWERS, BOUTONNIERES, AND CENTERPIECES
BRIDE $*

Flowers. Need I say more? Does it really matter to you if you have pansies instead of daises? Will you simply die without baby's breath? Enough said. Let her pick her flowers by herself. Let her pick all the flowers, including all the boutonnieres too.

Sometimes you may be required to pay for the groomsmen's and dads' boutonnieres, the bride's bouquet, and maybe the grandmothers' flowers. This may be a "tradition" in your area, and all eyes may look to you or your family to foot the bill. If this is the custom in your area (ask your fiancée or mother), make sure you don't get involved in the selection process—just fork over the cash to the appropriate party.

---

* Remember, "$" means that tradition dictates you, the groom, are responsible for forking over the cash and paying the tab.

The cummerbund should always be worn with the pleats facing upward. The original idea behind the cummerbund was to hold spare change and sometimes keys and theater tickets. This was so that your pants pockets wouldn't bulge. (You're getting married. It's your wedding day. You wouldn't want to give any of the bridesmaids an unwarranted thrill.) Make sure your bow tie is in front of the wings on your shirt and the boutonniere is worn on the left lapel of your jacket.

You know, I thought about covering the "finer points of tying a bow tie," but who the heck cares? Most bow ties are the pretied type, sort of clip-ons, used especially by tuxedo-rental shops. If you are fancy enough to buy an actual "tie bow tie," you probably already know how to tie one. Owning or renting a pretied bow tie is not the same as owning a clip-on regular tie. Don't worry, you won't be associated with trailer parks or inbreeding or anything like that.

YOUR TUX
BOTH OF YOU $

She has to look at you in the pictures for the rest of her life. Take her with you when you try on the tux and let her pick the one that she thinks looks the best on you. There are a lot of tux options, from full-dress tailcoats to cutaways to dinner jackets. Trust her judgment. She won't dress you up to look like a clown, and it won't kill you to be uncomfortable in a tux for one day.

You can either purchase or rent a tux. Unless you attend a vast number of formal events, it's not practical to purchase a tux. Personally, whether I'm in my Arnold Schwarzenegger weight-lifting mode or my Tom Arnold cheesecake à la mode, my weight fluctuates so much, it's safer for me to rent. If you purchase the tux, you may have to buy or rent a new cummerbund, tie, and shoes for each event you attend anyway.

It you rent, it's easier to rent in the town where you are having the wedding. The rental store is right there, and if there are any problems they can assist you immediately. If you rent out of town, you could be in trouble if your zipper breaks.

Your best man and groomsmen will be required to wear tuxes as well. Most of the major national tuxedo-rental shops will often offer the groom a free rental when his groomsmen rent from their store. It's advantageous to get fitted and order your tuxes as soon as you have your date, site, and reception finalized. Tux shops can sell out just as fast as catering halls. Your tux shop may be able to recommend a place for your groomsmen to be fitted in the town where they live, and they should send their measurements to the store ASAP. Sometimes the out-of-town store may require a small fee for this service. Make sure you have a professional measure you. If you measure yourself you could wind up with your tux looking like Payne Stewart's golf knickers.

WHAT IS A TROUSSEAU?

Trousseau comes from the French word *trousse*, or little bundle. In olden days, this was the clothing and linens that the bride brought with her to her new husband's home. It was expected to last at least a year. In later days, the trousseau came to mean dowries . . . enticements for the groom to marry the bride. Today, the trousseau is an excuse for the bride to shop for lingerie and honeymoon outfits. Of course, everything must be brand-new on your honeymoon. God forbid that one of the natives in that "Mosquito Coast" country where you are honeymooning sees her in an outfit she's worn before.

THE DRESSES
BRIDE

You can't see her wedding gown, and she probably won't tell you anything about it. Don't ask. You'll see it on your wedding day. Do you really want a say in the color and style of the bridesmaids' dresses? If so, stop here and begin reading again from the introduction.

Something old, something new, something borrowed, something blue . . . I haven't the slightest idea what the heck all this superstitious mumbo jumbo is about, but get used to this saying, since you'll be hearing it quite a bit! Don't worry, it doesn't have anything to do with you.

THE CAKE
BOTH OF YOU . . . Sort Of

Okay, now we are entering male territory . . . food. You can politely request the flavor of the cake. Don't get involved with the design and styling, just the flavor. One of the most important decisions a bride makes is choosing her wedding cake. Of course, there are endless possibilities, just like choosing her dress. This is another one of those sacred female affairs.

Almost every woman on the planet loves chocolate or some twisted concoction of it. Therefore, you may select any flavor your heart desires as long as it's chocolate something. Bakers even make white chocolate icing. You will find that there are virtually endless possibilities of cake flavors. You can both have fun with this. Most bakers will let you sample their creations, and many will make different layers of the cake different flavors.

Cake ideas:

- Double white chocolate
- Chocolate raspberry
- White chocolate lemon chiffon
- Chocolate truffle
- Chocolate mousse
- Chocolate almond fudge

THE GROOM'S CAKE

The groom's cake is a southern tradition
that's suddenly stylish. It's a single-layer cake
specifically designed for the groom. The groom's cake
can be fun. I recently heard of a bride surprising her hubby
with a groom's cake shaped like a Corvette, his favorite car.

SHOWERS AND PARTIES

You will continually be congratulated on your "good fortune" at becoming engaged. Strangers will smile and wish you well. Friends and family will want to throw parties. These parties can take a number of forms, and either you are invited or you are not invited to a party being thrown in honor of your engagement. Your fiancée may not have any showers or may have fifty; it depends on her friends and family and how "greedy" or "princessy" she is.

BRIDAL SHOWER

You're not invited. This party is only for the girls. Usually one of her bridesmaids, a close relative, or your mother will throw her the bridal shower. It's a shameless "showering" of girlie gifts. She will get "pretty" stuff for herself and for the house. They will giggle and complement each other on how skinny they each look, eat finger food, and dote over the newly engaged like she's Cinderella at the ball. You really don't want to be there!

BIRTH-CONTROL ALTERNATIVE . . . THE CAKE?

Okay, guys, unless you want a kid nine months after the wedding, don't let your wife cut the cake first. A ridiculous ancient superstition has it that the bride must cut the cake first. If she doesn't, the evil boogeyman puts a curse on her so that she will loose her fertility. I guess this could be a good alternative to birth control. Don't worry, most couples cut the cake together.

PERSONAL SHOWER

This is a takeoff on the bridal shower, and you're still not invited. This time she receives lingerie, dainty underwear, negligees, nighties, bath and honeymoon stuff, and lacy frilly things. Normally, a bunch of young ladies prancing around showing off their new lingerie is enough to excite any man. But remember, your mother may be there, her mother may be there, and don't forget your little sister and your ancient Aunt Bertha either. Enough to stop any arousing thought dead in its tracks.

COUPLE SHOWER

This is the politically correct version of the bridal shower. You *are* invited and may even get some household gifts. The couple shower tends to contain most of the elements of the bridal shower, complete with watercress finger sandwiches. They can sometimes be fun, but I would try to avoid them like the plague if I were you.

ENGAGEMENT PARTY

Often thrown by friends or family, the engagement party may be the last thing resembling a keg party you will see until well after you are married. All your friends and family that you *like* to party with are invited. Don't worry, your grandmother usually isn't invited, although there can be formal engagement parties where everyone is invited, including Great-Aunt Matilda. Guests are typically not required to give you gifts. Sometimes the engagement party can be a little awkward, since some of the people at the engagement party may not actually be invited to the wedding. For example, the annoying pain-in-the-ass guy from work says something like, "Gee whiz, this is the best party I have ever been to in my entire life. I can't wait until your wedding!" Yeah, right, you have no intention of inviting him to the wedding. Your dumb buddy who threw the engagement party invited your whole office, and this yutz showed up.

THE BACHELOR PARTY

Okay, guys, let's talk about the infamous bachelor party . . . the last chance for a single guy to have fun with all his buddies. Male bonding to the extreme. Testosterone raging. This is your time to have a blast before you strap on your "ball and chain."

You have heard the stories of the guy who has his bachelor party the night before the wedding and he shows up the next day totally hammered with the floozy he met the night before and she sits in the third row of the church. He passes out on the altar and his future Mrs. gets up and walks out, never to see him again.

Whether you drink and go to a topless bar, play cards, or just go to a movie, I have one thing to say: Is it worth it? Especially the night before the wedding?

Nothing will make your fiancée go crazier than the bachelor party. Girls talk about these things, and they fear them, simply because they don't understand them. They find the bachelor party to be male debauchery to the max. They see the party as a form of some antiwoman thing. Some fiancées may tell you to go out and have a good time; others are simply flat-out against it. You calm her down and try to explain to her that you will be home early. (Yeah, right.) You're with your best friends and family. This is your last day as a single guy. If you think the guys are going to let you leave early without a fight, you're sadly mistaken! A hangover can leave you and your wedding party with swollen, bloodshot eyes and a pale look. Some of you may be saying, "But I don't drink." That's fine, but if you're not accustomed to late nights out with the guys, you are going to feel the effects the day of your wedding. The pictures you'll take will last the rest of your life, and trust me, your wife is going to look at them often. The choice is yours. It's up to you.

The appropriate protocol for bachelor parties would dictate that you try to have the bachelor party at least a few days before the wedding to give you appropriate recovery time. In some cases, the wedding may be out of town or you may have buddies coming in from other areas; this can make it difficult to have a bachelor party a few days in advance of the wedding. I know that you don't plan your own bachelor party, but you must make it clear to your best man that the stag party should not be the night before the wedding and that if there is absolutely no other way than to have it the night before you will have to excuse yourself early. Make it clear to him. If he senses the slightest bit of hesitation in your voice he'll make sure you see the sun come up! No matter how much pressure your best man and friends may place on you about "partying till you puke," you will not be a "wimp" or even, much worse, "whipped" if you leave early. Remember, you will be a married man, and respecting the wishes of your wife is not wimpy in the least bit. It shows character and commitment. A properly planned bachelor party can be a memory of a lifetime. Don't make it the misery of your entire life!

Alternatives to the traditional bachelor party:

- Bachelor dinner at a restaurant
- Attend a sporting event or game (football, baseball, basketball, hockey)
- Fishing outing
- A day of golf (thirty-six holes)
- Camping trip
- Attend a rock concert

THE BACHELORETTE PARTY

Just remember, guys, if you can do it, she can too. Whatever you have done or will do, expect that she can and will do it as well. What's fair is fair. It may serve you both well to talk about the bachelor and bachelorette parties far in advance and discuss your plans to make sure that you are both comfortable with them.

THE REHEARSAL DINNER
GROOM (but Talk to Her About It) $

Now, here is where you get to shine. This baby is all yours. Go to town, but don't screw it up!

Relaxxx, take a deeeeep breath, and . . . callyourmotherasfastas-youcanbeggingforhelp! You need to discuss the rehearsal dinner with

your parents, close friends, and any other guy you know whose
wedding was in the same town where you will be getting married.
I know it's difficult for some guys to discuss these things and it makes
you feel wimpy, but it must be done. Before you have to pull out
your trusty yellow pages looking for banquet or church halls, ask
people about their experiences. Your wealthy Uncle Bob with the
big house on the hill may invite you to have the rehearsal dinner in
his home . . . which saves you money, and you don't even have to
clean up! Or, if you live in a large apartment building, they may have
facilities for just such an event. Many restaurants will have separate
rooms where you and your guests can elegantly dine in private.
Investigate.

The idea behind the rehearsal is to actually "practice" what you
are supposed to do at the wedding held the next day. After everyone
has their big laugh watching you screw up your lines, you eat . . .
on you!

Typically, the wedding party, the immediate family, the officiant,
their significant others, and anyone else who traveled from out of
town is invited to dinner. But if your best bud lives down the street,
invite him anyway. It's not, however, proper to invite people to the
rehearsal dinner who aren't invited to the wedding and the reception
the next day.

You can have a formal sit-down dinner or something as casual
as an outdoor barbecue or a six-foot sub. When you get closer to
locating the place, you can define the menu. Keep in mind that many
restaurants provide catering services. Shop around, since some catering
prices can be outrageous (baked beans to serve ten for $189). You
should dress appropriately, which means you really should wear a suit
(at least a tie), because your fiancée will probably be wearing a dress.
Remember, this is supposed to be a sacred, one-time event and you
should dress for the occasion. I know that you can't stand the damn
things and that you wear the monkey suits all week long and that

you don't want to wear one to *your* party. Wear a suit anyway: You are the guest of honor and host. Your guests can dress however you want them to, but remember, you will be on display. It won't kill you to put away the jeans for a night.

You will have to finalize the List of rehearsal-dinner attendees with your fiancée. With the invitations (remember the ones that you put stamps on?) make sure you include a separate RSVP card for all out-of-town guests, the wedding party, and any others who you would like to attend. Make sure that the List is finalized before you lick the envelopes. Base your rehearsal-dinner reservations on the number of people you invited, assuming 5 to 25 percent will not attend.

Ideas for sites for the rehearsal dinner:

- Banquet hall
- Church or synagogue hall
- Apartment building rec room
- Your house (if you must, but the last thing you want to do is throw a party at your house the day before your wedding; there are too many potential problems and you have to clean up)
- Your parents' house
- A friend or relative's house
- A restaurant
- Stay away from bars (see "The Bachelor Party" earlier in this chapter)

HELPFUL TIP:
Don't play any drinking games at your rehearsal dinner or at the reception. Minus brownie points.

OPEN OR CASH BAR? APPLIES TO THE REHEARSAL DINNER AND THE RECEPTION
BOTH OF YOU $

I'm on my soapbox again. Bars can cause a lot of strife at weddings. Your religion may forbid alcohol consumption or her parents may be totally against it and not allow drinking at their child's wedding. Meanwhile, you were the beer-bong champ of your fraternity and can't get by at formal parties without your trusty six-pack of "genuine," imported from Milwaukee, domestic beer. Some parents may not want to pay for alcohol. You will have a lot of decisions to make and may end up paying for the booze yourselves.

I have attended weddings where I was required to pay for my drinks. Forgetting college, think of the bar this way: Would you invite friends over to your house for a party and make them pay for their drinks? Probably not, unless you are a major tightwad. Why then would you make people pay for the booze at your wedding?

Open-bar alternatives if cost is an issue:

- Serve champagne and wine. Have the wait staff walk around with bottles of champagne and wine. Usually people will not switch from champagne or wine to liquor, which helps keep the costs down.
- Offer only beer and wine and one glass of champagne for a toast. Do not offer any liquor.
- Close the bar during dinner.

Sometimes the facility may allow you to purchase your own booze for the rehearsal and the reception. Often they may charge you a handling fee or cork fee, so be sure you check beforehand for details.

If you have bartenders and wait staff at the rehearsal dinner, you are required to tip them 15 percent or more if it is not already included in your contract.

THE LIMO
GROOM $

Determine how many limousines you want, if any at all. Typically, you will need at least one limo for you and your wife. She takes the limo from her home to the ceremony, and you both ride in it to the reception after you're married. The wedding party can ride with you from the ceremony to the reception, and the bride's parents and your parents may also have a limo, but these are totally optional.

Again, consult the yellow pages. Use the same exercise from Chapter 2: Investigate, Establish Common Criteria, Compare. Decide on the color of the limo, the number of people it has to seat, and the total time it's needed and start calling.

It is customary to tip the limo driver 15 percent of the total bill if it's not included in your contract.

Alternatives to the limo:

- Horse-drawn carriage
- Trolley car
- Your own car
- Borrow a friend's new car
- Rent an exotic sports or luxury car and have the best man drive

MARRIAGE LICENSE
BOTH OF YOU $

You are required by law to get a marriage license. Each state has its own rules and regulations. Some states require that you take a blood test. Others require that there be a cooling-off period, just like with handguns. You know how deadly passion and a set of blue balls can be!

You will have to get a license in the state where the nuptials will be performed and not where you live now! Make sure to check with the county office in the state where you will be getting married several months in advance to make sure you understand the licensing requirements. You will both have to be present when you apply for the license; be sure that you arrive in town prior to the cooling-off period. You are typically required to pay for it, so make sure you know how much it costs. Some states won't take a personal check, so have cash.

If you are getting married overseas you have another set of problems and requirements. Your travel agent can help or should at least point you in the right direction.

"Our custom of having the bride leave her home and family and come to live with her new husband would seem strange to the old North American Indians, the Eskimos of Baffin Bay and the Firelanders of Cape Horn. There, the bride never left home, but her husband moved in with her and his mother-in-law."

—from Frank Klock, *Apes and Husbands*

PICTURES AND VIDEOS
BRIDE $

Choosing a photographer and/or videographer can be like flipping a coin. Your fiancée may see pictures from other weddings, or her girlfriend may recommend someone. But if the "professional" took fantastic pictures at one wedding, it doesn't mean your pictures are going to be great. To ensure that you have the best possible pictures and video, define exactly what you want before the big day.

Don't arbitrarily leave it up to the photographer or videographer. Any special requests, such as a photo of your pookie bear and her Great–Aunt Ethel or one of you and your high school football buddies, must be put in writing. Give the photographer a list of all the photos you want taken throughout the day. If you don't know the shots that you'll need, ask the pro. I have provided you with a photographer and videographer checklist in Chapter 6.

> **At a friend's recent wedding, the "professional" photographer forgot to take a picture of the groom with his immediate family and the "professional" videographer spelled the bride's name wrong on the video.**
>
> **These problems should have been avoided.**

Some key shots:

- Bride at home
- Bride getting into car and/or out of car
- Bride coming down aisle
- Father giving bride away
- Groom and groomsmen at altar (or in procession)
- Bridesmaids coming down aisle
- Parents coming down aisle
- Groom meeting bride at altar
- Exchanging vows
- The kiss
- The lighting of the unity candle
- Bride and groom posed at altar
- Bride and/or groom with parents, grandparents, best man, maid of honor, wedding party, or any other relatives or friends

- Bride and groom leaving ceremony
- Bride and groom arriving at reception
- The receiving line
- Parents, grandparents, stepparents, and any other relatives or friends
- Buffet, dessert, and/or cookie table
- The cake table
- Bride and groom at their table
- Head table
- Parents' table
- Bride and groom cutting cake
- Bride and groom feeding each other cake
- Bride and groom toasting
- Bride and groom's first dance
- Bride dancing with her father
- Groom dancing with his mother
- Bride and groom dancing with in-laws
- Best man giving toast
- Groom taking off bride's garter
- Garter toss and bouquet toss
- Bride and groom leaving reception

RECEPTION

BRIDE

This is the biggie. You'll need to find a place for the reception, choose the menu and drinks, do seating arrangements, and more.

Your fiancée will have to do the bulk of the reception planning. First, she is responsible for locating and procuring the reception hall. I'm warning you now, she may require that you visit a few of these places to talk with the management and taste the food. Invoke your

"Right of First Refusal" rule and have her narrow down her choices to two locations. Then take the time to visit the locations. Both of you should decide on the reception site.

It can be kind of awkward and tends to be a little tacky, but most reception halls will allow you to attend other weddings so you can see how well they perform (the reception facility, not the bride and groom). You're basically crashing someone else's wedding. If anyone asks what you're doing there, say you're with the groom. Also, make sure you dress appropriately—you're at someone's wedding . . . you can't wear jeans! (Yup, a suit again.)

The food issues for the reception will be similar to the issues you faced with the rehearsal dinner, except I don't think your fiancée will go for a six-foot sub. Typically, the reception will be either buffet or a formal sit-down dinner. I preferred a buffet. This way, I figured, my buddies and I could eat as much as we wanted. However, that was not elegant enough for snookums. No matter how many "Rights of First Refusal" I tried to invoke, I was denied. Her father and brothers even lobbied her on my behalf (after all, they are hungry guys too). I wasn't even allowed to have a dessert buffet. Apparently, she'd always wanted a sit-down dinner so . . . formal sit-down it was. For larger weddings you almost have to have a buffet. Take it if you can, guys. In the end it won't matter anyway, since you will be pulled in fifty directions and won't get a chance to eat much of anything.

Your choice of food will, in many cases, be dictated by the ethnicity of the families involved. Italian families have Italian foods. Jewish families have Jewish. Greeks have Greek. The Irish have beer. Choosing the menu should be fun. Don't stress about the food. In many cases the reception halls will allow you to sample the dishes before you commit to a specific menu.

The seating arrangements can be a major issue of contention among guests. Cousin Joey got seated at a better table than Uncle

Guido. Make a list, check it twice, don't put naughty with nice. You know who would work well with whom.

Unless you have an even number of people on each side, splitting the bride's side off to the left and the groom's to the right doesn't always work well. Have fun, mix and match. We're all one big happy family now, so everyone may as well get to know each other. Work this out with your fiancée and consult others as little as possible. Every person you ask will give you a different opinion about the seating arrangement. (Remember Great-Aunt Matilda who hates Cousin Myron?)

In the Middle Ages, Christian "tradition" said that the bride and her family and friends were on the left side and that the groom and his clan were on the right side. The groom had the bride stand to his left so that in case of an attack from roving bandits, or if someone tried to "steal" his bride, he could quickly brandish his sword. (In the Middle Ages it was assumed everyone was right-handed.) Therefore, the bride always stood to her husband's left so she could be protected. Hence, the bride's family sits to the left, the groom's to the right. Sword in the right hand . . . mother-in-law to the left . . . okay, guys, I know what you are thinking. Forget it! Don't get any crazy ideas of chopping up her mother just yet!

THE BAND OR DJ
BOTH OF YOU

When planning my wedding, I initially thought that I would choose all the music. I'm into music, have the killer Alpine stereo in my car with dual rear speakers and heavy bass. I knew I was capable of picking the music. How wrong I was.

There are two ways to have music at your wedding reception: a band or a DJ. Bands can take many forms, shapes, and sizes, from traditional Gaelic folk music to a jazz or blues ensemble to Tony Romo's Sizzling New York Wedding Sounds. I've heard people say, "Unless you have a band, your wedding is tacky." Well, have you heard most of the wedding bands out there? They never excited me. They completely butcher most songs, and there are only so many renditions of "New York, New York" I can take. My wife originally wanted a band, but I invoked the "Right of First Refusal," and she concurred. We opted for a DJ. With a DJ, I knew exactly what I was getting. You give the DJ a list of the exact songs you want and he plays them. No mystery. Plus, it's less expensive and usually adds more variety. I even told the DJ that if he played just one "Electric Slide," "Hokey Pokey," or "Chicken Dance" I would break his legs and not pay him a cent. He happily complied with my wishes. All right, I admit it, I'm guilty. I did let him play one stinking "Macarena."

After I'd phonetically spelled out all the names for the emcee at my wedding, the putz still mispronounced my mother's name. He called her Ellen instead of Elaine. The guy looked like a big fool.

Most DJs will provide you with a list of popular songs appropriate for weddings that you can choose from. Well, I went through the list and circled my favorites only to have my fiancée go back, erase my choices, and reselect the romantic "proper" songs for our wedding. All told, I got about five picks. Guys, let her have her lovey-dovey stuff. It's only one day. You can bring your Walkman on the honeymoon.

An excellent alternative to a band is to have a string quartet play during the ceremony and dinner and have a DJ do the dancing music afterward. We hired a string quartet made up of college music majors and they were great. They were the hit of the day, very professional for college kids, and well worth the money.

Whether you have a band, a DJ, or a string quartet, someone from the group typically acts as the master of ceremonies (MC, or emcee). This doesn't have to be anything more than knowing the flow of your wedding, when dinner will be served, when the cake will be cut, when you will have the first dance, and so on. If you are going to be announced as a couple with your wedding party and parents, make sure that the emcee can phonetically pronounce the names. Make the emcee repeat the names to you a number of times.

Just like you did when researching the reception, interview the bands, DJs, or whomever you are considering to perform at your reception, and make sure they can do a good job. Hear them play or at least ask if they have a demo tape you can review. There is absolutely nothing wrong with seeing them in action.

The DJ at Bill's wedding came up to the bride and groom as the reception was beginning and asked them to pick another song for their first dance. (Guys, you know how important the special first-dance song is!) He said he didn't have the one they wanted. An usher quickly went to the bride's apartment to get the cassette tape so that they could have "their" song for the first dance as husband and wife.

MORAL OF THE STORY:
Make sure, in advance, the DJ or band can
play any specially requested songs.

Inappropriate wedding songs:

- "Why Don't We Get Drunk (and Screw)," Jimmy Buffett
- "White Wedding," Billy Idol
- "To All the Girls I've Loved Before," Julio Iglesias and Willy Nelson
- "Paradise by the Dashboard Light (Praying for the End of Time)," Meat Loaf

CHOOSING YOUR BEST MAN AND GROOMSMEN (USHERS)

GROOM $

You have to decide whom you want to be your best man and your groomsmen. If in doubt, the safest course is to choose family members. If she has brothers you may want to consider having them as groomsmen, even if you don't like them. This is wonderful in-law PR and gets you major brownie points with your future wife and her family. Typically, you want to pick the same number of grooms-men as bridesmaids. This isn't always possible and that's okay; you can have an odd number of people. A good rule of thumb is that there should be one usher for every fifty guests.

Traditionally, it's your responsibility to pay for the lodging of your best man and your groomsmen. If you can put them up at your house, at a family member's house, or at a friend's, great. If not, and they must stay at a hotel, it is your responsibility to pay for their hotel room and taxes. Nothing more. They pay for their tux rentals, their hotel bar tab, and their pay-per-view dirty movies.

Remember, your best man will be required to make a speech and arrange the bachelor party. Pick your best man accordingly.

PARTNER IN CRIME

In the old days your bride was "stolen" from the next village. Your assistant during the "raid," the guy who watched your back and helped hide you after you successfully "stole" your bride, later became known as the best man.

RESPONSIBILITIES OF THE BEST MAN

Most wedding-etiquette books and magazines that your fiancée has piling up give totally antiquated information regarding the best man. It seems like their info is from 1802. They say hilarious things like, "It is the responsibility of the best man to help you dress for the wedding." My brother was my best man, and I'll be damned if I let him help me put on my pants—straighten a tie maybe, although Mom is probably better suited for that. They also say the best man should "remind you to order your flowers and to obtain a marriage license." Are you kidding me? My brother telling me not to forget the flowers? This is a joke, right? According to these books and magazines, the best man is supposed to arrange the honeymoon as well. I don't know about you, but I would hate to see where my brother would send me! One book even said that the best man should help the groom get undressed after the wedding and then help him get into his travel clothes. If I didn't want him touching me before the wedding, why the hell should he touch me after? In addition, he is supposed to protect your luggage and car from pranks. At most weddings that I've ever attended, the best man was usually the ringleader of the pranks.

Most best men will have a hell of a time with the speech, let alone all the other responsibilities that "tradition" dictates. I recommend keeping the duties of the best man to a minimum. The person who should handle all your running around is the "point man." (The next section in this chapter explains about the "point man.")

As a safer bet, the best man should be responsible for:

- The toast
- Signing the marriage license and holding onto it for safekeeping
- Holding onto the wedding bands before the service
- Making sure that he is dressed, in his tux, and at the festivities at the appropriate times
- Arranging the bachelor party (and not the night before the wedding!)
- Assisting with transportation arrangements to and from the ceremony
- Keeping the wedding party in line

Keys to a good piece of toast:

- Always stand when giving the toast
- Tell a personal story about the bride and groom
- Humor usually works
- Don't read the toast
- Be sincere
- Talk about the couple and their relationship
- Don't talk about all the girls the groom bonked and how lucky the bride was to land him
- Don't talk about how the groom won't "come out and play" anymore
- Never mention anything "ball and chain" related
- Keep it short and sweet

"POINT MAN"

Traditionally, the best man is the "point man" or "go-to guy" at the rehearsal, wedding, and the reception. He is supposed to assist you with anything you need. Most best men have such an active role in the wedding ceremony and must psych themselves up so much to give the toast that they can be virtually useless to you for other things. Therefore, you will need someone to handle your miscellaneous chores. Your fiancée should have a "point lady" to handle all her errands as well. Typically, the maid of honor will serve as her "point lady." The maid of honor usually understands what is required of her and will assume the necessary duties, so your fiancée won't typically need another "point lady." Don't have either father act as your "point man," since they will have too much to do. Make sure that your "point man" is someone you can trust, who is responsible and can take charge, and who can handle things smoothly without bothering you. I recommend appointing a groomsman or a close relative or friend as your "point man." Make him responsible for paying any of the fees or tips due and have him collect and keep track of your gifts, cards, and, most important, your money envelopes. If your "point man" is a groomsman, make him responsible for keeping the wedding party in line and ensuring that everyone knows what they have to do and where they have to be. He should also assist the best man in arranging the transportation for the wedding party and the parents, if a limo is not available. Have the "point man" hold your keys and travel tickets. If there are any problems, he needs to deal with them and not involve either you or your new wife. For example, Uncle Eddie didn't receive his complimentary party favor from the reception hall, which consists of two pieces of chocolate with a few almonds, and he is having a cow. You shouldn't have to go and discuss this with the caterer; it's the "point man's" job. Remember, your fiancée may harbor desires for perfection and may freak out if presented with problems during the day. Keep the problems away from both of you as much as possible so you can enjoy everything.

If your "point man" is not an usher, make sure that you get him a gift as well.

Provide the "point man" with lists and a detailed "playbook" highlighting the exact instructions of what will take place.

This includes:

- A list of all pictures required of the photographer and videographer
- A list of required tips to be paid
- An itinerary of events
- A seating chart
- A list of all vendors with their home and work telephone numbers
- The "playbook"

RESPONSIBILITIES OF THE GROOMSMEN (USHERS)

Typically, the major responsibility of groomsmen is to escort guests to their appropriate seats at the ceremony. An usher should escort a lady down the aisle on his right arm. If they are accompanied by a guy, have him follow behind. A groomsman shouldn't offer his arm to a man unless the gentleman is elderly and in need of assistance. Other than "offering an arm," the groomsmen should just look "pretty" for the pictures and have fun. They will have to dance a little bit, play Mr. Politician, shake hands, and talk to your relatives, but that's about it.

GIFTS FOR THE WEDDING PARTY, PARENTS, AND YOUR NEW BRIDE

BOTH OF YOU $

GROOMSMEN

When most guys hear that they have to give their groomsmen a gift the first thing that comes to mind is: a nice pen set, an engraved pewter beer mug, a tie clip, a money clip . . . you get the idea. How many guys do you know who drink out of engraved pewter mugs, or use tie clips and money clips? Very few. Most of the time these gifts sit on a mantle or in a drawer collecting dust.

You don't have to be run-of-the-mill. Get your ushers something that they will use and possibly cherish. I can't tell you how many pen sets I have received from being a groomsman. Sure I like them, they're okay. But to be honest, I don't even remember who they came from. You don't have to spend a fortune—just be creative. I was given an excellent gift recently. It's a personal pocket computer. It was a very inexpensive Radio Shack model. I store all my telephone numbers, addresses, and appointments in it. I use it every day and will never forget who gave it to me. You wouldn't believe how many pewter mugs I have that have never even seen a beer. Another great idea is getting the groomsmen two tickets each to a major sporting event.

TALK ABOUT A WEDDING PRESENT!

"Among the Zande of Central Africa a younger brother had access to his older brother's wife, whom he will eventually inherit anyway. Married Zande men could also sleep with their own wives' younger sisters and with their younger brother's wives, with permission."

—from G. Robina Quale, *A History of Marriage Systems*

BRIDESMAIDS—Bride

See earlier section about flowers. Let her pick out the girls' stuff.

PARENTS' GIFTS

If your parents or the bride's parents have just shelled out a big chunk of change for the wedding, there is not much monetarily that you can ever do to compensate them. So don't think in those terms. Get the parents something they can remember and keep. My wife picked out two "poem-type things" for the parents and had them framed. When the parents read them at the rehearsal dinner, there wasn't a dry eye in the place. They now have them hanging in their living rooms. Other great gift ideas for the parents are purchasing them a wedding album or providing them with an engraved picture frame just waiting for your wedding picture.

You can present the gifts any time after the start of the rehearsal dinner. The rehearsal dinner is probably the only quality time you will have to present the gifts to the bridal party and family members before leaving for your honeymoon.

FOR YOUR NEW WIFE

Exchanging gifts with your new bride is not mandatory. Talk to her about it and see if she wants to exchange gifts. Chances are that you may want to save the money since you're now starting a new life together and bills will pile up quickly. You should agree on the amount you will spend on each other and, if you do exchange presents, get her something sentimental and romantic.

Instead of buying gifts for each other, some couples put that money toward the wedding bands, honeymoon, or new house. Heck, she got the engagement ring already, what more does she want?

Gift ideas for your wife:

- Honeymoon
- Wedding bands
- Any jewelry
- Cedar chest
- Music or jewelry box

THE WEDDING BANDS
(NOT THE MUSIC, STUPID, THE RINGS)
BOTH OF YOU $

To be on the safe side, you should purchase your wedding bands about three months before the wedding. The wedding bands won't cost you near the amount you spent on the engagement ring. The retail shop where you purchased the engagement ring is probably a good bet for the wedding bands. Here again, you will have your choice of styles and metals (gold, platinum, or, to a lesser extent, silver). For brownie points you could suggest to your fiancée that you have something inscribed on the inside of the rings. It could be a romantic saying (sorry, can't be of any help with that), the date you were engaged, or the date of your wedding with your married initials.

Remember, the K is for karat, which refers to the purity of gold. Twenty-four karat is essentially pure gold, or twenty-four parts gold. You would think that 24K is the way to go for the wedding bands . . . wrong; 24K is just too pure and considered too soft for practical use. Therefore, for the gold to be strong enough to wear on your finger it must be combined with other metals to strengthen it for use and abuse on your finger. Eighteen karat is eighteen parts gold and six parts other metals, 14K is fourteen parts gold and ten parts other metals, and 10K is ten parts gold and fourteen other. Anything less than ten parts cannot be called gold and is typically referred to as gold plated or gold filled. Make sure that the real gold you purchase, whether 18K, 14K, or 10K, is stamped with the K, or karat mark. If it doesn't have the mark it's probably not real gold.

Guys tend to be divided along battle lines over wearing the wedding ring (choker, nose ring, ball and chain—fill in your own phrase to describe the wedding band). Some don't mind wearing their band; others wouldn't be caught dead with one on. It is definitely up to you. This is another one of those issues that you'd better discuss with your fiancée. She will probably expect you to wear the ring without question. If that's not your style, you'd better tell her so. If you take it off after you are married and don't wear it, it could very well mean World War III. Of course, major brownie points if you wear the ring.

BRIDAL REGISTRY
BRIDE (but You Can Help)

If you're like most guys, you can't stand shopping unless it's for power tools, automotive stuff, or sporting goods. Well, guess what? Get ready, because your lovely honey bunch will want to drag you to all the department stores at your local mall trying to find the perfect shop for you to register for bridal gifts. She will tell you that these gifts are for you too, and that you have to help her pick them out and must go with her to register.

This whole concept confused me at first. I always thought people gave you gifts that they wanted to give you, not gifts that you told them to give to you. How wrong I was! You go to a store, pick out the merchandise you want, put it on a list, then have relatives and friends tell all your guests where you are registered, and the guests buy you the gifts from your list! This is great. Where was this registry list for birthdays and Christmases when I was a kid? Although everyone knows and accepts the bridal-registry concept, it is still not "approved of" to list your registry place on your invitations. Tell me that makes sense? The bridal registry informs your guests of exactly what to buy, but it's a major no-no to write it on your invitations . . . go figure.

Bridal registering can be extremely boring and tedious. But it can also be fun, almost making you feel like a kid in a candy store. I would recommend that you have your fiancée pick the store and choose the majority of the gifts. Invoke "Right of First Refusal" powers. Let her select everything she wants. Do you really want to pick out china patterns, towels, pots and pans, sheets and comforters? I didn't. But most department stores have sporting goods, automotive, and appliance departments. I had a field day.

Another thing I don't understand is the concept of getting gifts of fine china for your wedding. My parents got fine china. Her parents got fine china. Our grandparents got fine china. They never used it. Now we have two sets of antique fine china that were given to us. Why girls have to pick out "more" china I'll never know. It's not practical. It's not like we ever have formal dinners at the house. I'm so clumsy that I've already broken half of it. I'm sure you all will agree. Times have changed since the *Leave It to Beaver* days. I don't think your new wife will be scrubbing toilets around the house wearing a dress, high heels, and pearls. She probably won't have slippers and a cold drink waiting for you, her husband and sole provider, when you return home from a hard day's work and bless her with your presence. And I'm sure she won't be serving any fast-food burgers on the finest china either.

In addition to the items you registered for, you will receive untold numbers of candlesticks, picture frames, vases, and drinking glasses of all sizes and shapes. Sometimes it seems like these gifts are recycled from one wedding to the next. Expect it and then try to return them. Not even the stores want them back!

Today, many major department stores will have bridal registries listed on their countrywide internal computer system or on the World Wide Web (WWW) so that your guests will be able to access your registry from anywhere. If you have a lot of guests traveling to your wedding it may be easier for them if you register with a national department-store chain since many have branches or affiliates in most states. Make sure you check the return policy of the store where you register.

"The American [groom] can consider himself lucky in receiving a host of valuable wedding gifts from his bride's family . . . Many primitive peoples require that the groom enter a long indentured service to the bride's family without pay, during which time he is given the roughest treatment possible as a test of character and skill. Only at the conclusion of his probationary period, which may last for years, does he gain his independence and full possession of his wife."

—from Frank Klock, *Apes and Husbands*

Alternatives to the traditional bridal registry:

- Hardware store: If you will be combining both households you may not need sheets, but you could sure use that new hammer, wallpaper, and paint.
- Honeymoon registry: You register with your travel agent and people contribute money toward your honeymoon.
- Furniture registry: Many better furniture stores have recently begun offering bridal registries. You may also be able to register for furniture at a department store.

- Mortgage registry: If you are thinking of buying a house, check with your mortgage lender to see if they have a registry program set up. Recently, the Office of Housing of the U.S. Department of Housing and Urban Development (HUD) set up a mortgage registry for newlyweds. Your local Federal Housing Administration lender applies your cash gifts toward a down payment on a house. Call your local HUD office or FHA lender for more info.
- Sporting goods stores.
- Book, video, or music stores.

THE FINE PRINT
BOTH OF YOU $

PRENUPTIAL AGREEMENT

I told you in the beginning I wasn't messing around. I hate to say it, but prenups are definite minus brownie points, and the minus points can be significant. Prenups are minus brownie points simply because people don't understand them. Most people feel the prenup is some evil concoction developed by fancy lawyers to leave an innocent wife destitute when her billionaire husband decides to dump her for a twenty-two-year-old bimbo. TV, of course, has perpetuated this image.

Why would you want to have a prenuptial agreement? I'm not a lawyer (and don't want to be one), but here goes.

Prenups are valuable in the following situations:

- They spell out ownership of property at the time of marriage.
- They can protect the property rights for your children from a previous marriage in the cases of divorce or death.

- They can determine the financial responsibilities of each person.
- They protect the future rights of each person.
- They protect the interest of a family business.
- They address how you divide property and responsibilities during and, if necessary, after the marriage.

If you hang with "The Donald" or were featured on *Lifestyles of the Rich and Famous,* you'd better speak with your lawyer. For most of us, however, prenups may not be necessary. (I say that, but 50 percent of all couples that get married today will end up divorced . . . how sad.) Typically, prenups are utilized by couples who are not marrying for the first time or who have "significant" assets. It's always recommended that both parties have lawyers draw up the contract.

Many times the prenup can be drawn up with a "sunset" clause, which states that the prenup, or certain clauses in it, will be void after a specific period of time has elapsed.

NEW DEFINITION OF INSURANCE?

"The Subanum of Mindanao in the Philippines . . . expect the household of a deceased spouse of either sex to provide a new spouse."

—from G. Robina Quale, *A History of Marriage Systems*

WILL AND INSURANCE

You're going to be married soon. What happens if you get run over by a Mack truck a month after you are married? Who takes care of your wife now that you have just loaded her up with $20,000 of extra bills from the wedding and honeymoon, not to mention your funeral? How does the mortgage get paid? What about the business you owned? Does your wife get every bit of it or do you let all your greedy relatives fight it out in court? These could be real issues, so make sure you have all your bases covered. Get a will and insurance.

> "Among the Kirgiz of Siberia . . . the husband merely had to say, I divorce thee, three times to rid himself of his spouse. He was careful about uttering these words and finding himself without both wife and cattle."
>
> —from Frank Klock, *Apes and Husbands*

HONEYMOON PLANNING
GROOM (but She Can Help) $

This is my favorite part. Honeymoon planning can actually be fun. With all the stresses of preparation and the actual wedding, you and your future wife will need a well-deserved break. There is nothing better than a nice loooonnnggg honeymoon. Have a talk with your fiancée and tell her that this is your baby. Chances are, she will even let you do it.

You will be responsible for paying for this one, so it'll be the shopping exercise from Chapter 2 again: Investigate, Establish Common Criteria, Compare. Your first job is to determine your budget. If you only have $1,000 to spend on a honeymoon, it will not get you much of a luxury European vacation for two. Next, you must determine the geographic location of where you want to go: Florida, the Caribbean, Hawaii, Mexico, Europe, a cruise, or a long weekend for two in the Poconos, complete with heart-shaped bed, mirrors on the ceiling, and the champagne-glass–shaped Jacuzzi. Your local bookstore and library will have ample resources, not to mention the excellent resources I have included for you in Chapter 6. Believe it or not, the bridal magazines that your fiancée has piling up in the corner are also good resources for your honeymoon. Look in the back of the magazines. They'll provide information about different destinations and will list toll-free telephone numbers. Another good resource is the Sunday travel section of a major newspaper. (Pick the large city nearest to you, and buy its paper. The *New York Times* has a great travel section.) The travel section will usually list special package deals and promotions available. Third, determine how long you want your honeymoon to last (forever and ever, every day is our honeymoon . . . my wife made me say that) and block out the dates that you can take it. Make sure you both check your work schedules. If you only get one week of vacation a year, it can make an extended honeymoon almost impossible.

Okay, you have chosen the place and the type of vacation, have a budget, and have picked the date you plan to leave and the number of days you can stay. Now get that trusty, worn and tattered phone book out and start calling your local travel agents. A great travel agent can be invaluable, but quite often different agents offer different promotions and know of different deals. It may be a good idea to talk with a few different agents.

You may find after doing some research that you had unrealistic expectations about how much a honeymoon will cost. Re-evaluate. You may still be able to go to that exotic locale, but for fewer days and you may have to stay in a less expensive hotel. Book the honeymoon well in advance so that you are guaranteed reservations and maybe even a better price. Make sure you get a written itinerary from your travel agent.

Things may be hectic at the office and you may not be able to get all the time off that you want; or maybe you had to pay for your own wedding and money is tight right now, so you're thinking about postponing the honeymoon until a later date. That's fine, but the problem is that you only really have one honeymoon, and that comes right after your wedding. Yeah, sure, you can call the trip you take a year later your honeymoon, but it's not the same thing. It's just . . . another trip, not the honeymoon. The honeymoon is a great experience, spending your first few days as a married couple together, relaxing and enjoying each other's company. Try to make every effort to get away if you can. If you can't afford anything fancy, stay with your Great-Uncle Irving, who lives in the Leisure Village Senior Retirement Community in south Florida for a few days. At least it's warm and you will be spending some quality time with your new wife, relaxing on the beach. Big deal, so you have to go to early-bird dinners with your uncle and listen to him complain about his infrequent bowel movements and herniated disk. It's still your honeymoon!

ALL-INCLUSIVES

There are a number of resorts in the United States and abroad that offer all-inclusive holidays. This means that you pay one large fee at the beginning and then pay for nothing (room, food, various activities and tours, or sometimes even drinks) while you are vacationing. Many of these all-inclusives are top-notch resorts with world-class cuisine. All-inclusives are a good way to keep unexpected costs low.

CRUISING

My wife suggested that for at least part of our honeymoon we should go on a cruise. I hemmed and hawed but told her I would investigate a little. I tend to get very hyper if kept confined for an extended period of time and was worried that I would feel cooped up on a cruise ship. I like to have the ability to come and go as I please. My wife and the travel agent assured me that there was plenty to do . . . and plenty to eat . . . on the cruise ship. They were right! I didn't get bored and I broke all previous dessert-eating records aboard ship. Fourteen in one day! We paid one price and I never had to pull out my wallet for anything except drinks and our shore excursions. We visited five exotic ports and my wife didn't even get seasick. There are always cruise deals, so check with your travel agent and the Sunday travel section of your paper.

PASSPORT AND OTHER TRAVEL ISSUES

Many foreign nations require that you have a valid passport before entering their country. If you don't have a passport, make sure you apply for one as soon as possible. The passport office is government run, so expect delays. It's important that on your passport, your driver's license, and your airplane or cruise tickets your name appears exactly the same way. This probably will not affect you, but it could affect your fiancée. I know you both may be anxious to have her assume your last name, but it can screw up international travel. The customs guy at the "Mosquito Coast" country may not give a crap that you were just married and that "Mary Jane Smith" is the same person as "Mary Jane Jones." He may still throw both of you in a dark room and rummage through your wife's silky underwear and negligees. It could ruin a great vacation. You may even have a problem at a U.S. airport with today's strict security if the names are different.

REQUIREMENTS FOR OBTAINING A U.S. PASSPORT

You can obtain the proper DSP-11 passport form from your local clerk of courts or designated U.S. post offices. For a nonrush passport allow twenty-five business days, but this is the U.S. government at its best, so realistically give yourself a few months.

1. Proof of citizenship. Can be a certified birth certificate. Hospital records are not accepted.

2. Two photos (make sure they conform with passport rules and regulations).

3. Proof of ID. Must be a picture ID. Can be a driver's license or student ID.

4. $60 passport fee for anyone over fifteen years of age.

5. Add $35 for a rush passport if your airplane or ship is leaving within ten days.

6. Sign the DSP-11 passport form.

MOVING IN

You have been so consumed with keeping your fiancée sane during the wedding planning, have you given any thought to where you are going to live? Are you currently living together? Will you stay where you are? Will you move in with her? She with you? Are you going to buy a house or find another apartment? Live with the in-laws to save money? Will you move in together before or after the wedding?

Since couples are marrying much older today than in the Stone Ages of your parents' time, most couples have established households already. If you haven't officially moved in together, you need to consider how you are going to combine all the stuff you both have accumulated. It's a good idea to take inventory of the things that each of you have and make a list of things you need. The necessities can be added to your bridal registry.

Moving in inevitably brings stress. Like a couple of wild dogs, you will stake out and mark your territory. She may want to throw out your favorite recliner that you bought from a secondhand store ten years ago for your dorm room. You refuse to let her put her collection of ballet posters on the walls. Are you really going to do the decorating? Do you really care in which drawer she places the silverware? I was in the furniture business for a long time and didn't even do the bulk of the decorating in our house. Work it out and try to compromise—it's not worth fighting over. Make your wife feel comfortable in her new home. When it comes to things like putting pink curtains in your bedroom, you may have to invoke your "Right of First Refusal," but if it is not that big a deal invite her to make your new home wonderful.

I know we are in the "politically correct era and at the start of a new millennium," and men and women are supposed to share household responsibilities equally, but when it comes to the home it is still predominantly the woman's responsibility. It doesn't matter that she is a high-powered VP for a billion-dollar company and she works sixty hours a week; society still dictates that the house is her responsibility. There are househusbands, and I have been one from time to time, but even though my wife moved into my home, it automatically became hers. When people come over to visit and the house is a mess, it is a reflection of both of you, but mostly her. People will look at her as if she's not doing her "womanly" duties, while you were the slob who didn't clean up the mess you made in the first place.

PERSONAL FINANCES

You're in love right now and caught up in the bliss of getting married. Well, what happens afterward when all the bills come due? Listed below are financial questions that should be addressed sooner than later. Neither of you will want any financial surprises after your wedding high wears off. Go through the list and discuss these questions with your fiancée.

- How will the bills be paid?
- From where will the money come?
- Who will actually write out the checks?
- Who will keep the family budget?
- Will you keep a joint checking account or separate checking accounts?
- If you keep separate accounts will each of you be able to sign on the other's account?
- Have you thought about establishing savings and investments?
- What about life insurance?
- Do you both have health insurance?
- Do you have a will?
- How will you pay the past debts each of you have incurred (credit cards, student loans)?
- Are you aware of each other's credit situation?
- How many credit cards do you each have and what are the balances?
- What major purchases will you need to make in the near future? Do you have a washer and dryer, refrigerator, furniture, a car, and whatever else you'll need?
- How will you pay for these major purchases?

CHAPTER 4

SHOWTIME! THE REHEARSAL AND THE WEDDING

What's the difference between an in-law and an outlaw?
Outlaws are wanted!

THE REHEARSAL AND REHEARSAL DINNER

This is your last chance to work out all the kinks. The pregame walk-through. You go through the motions to make sure you know exactly what you are doing. Try to relax. You will have a lot to re-member, so you need to concentrate, but have fun. Your fiancée, the officiant, the maid of honor, and the best man are there to help you remember what you are doing and point you in the right direction. On second thought, forget the best man, he's worthless—he's still worrying about giving the damn toast. Go with the flow. No one will know or care if you walk down the aisle too fast or stand instead of kneel (except for the bride, of course).

The rehearsal dinner is the perfect time to chill out and relax with the bridal party, your immediate family, and the out-of-town guests. It's also the most opportune time for you to hand out the gifts for the bridal party and parents. Remember, you can't see the bride after midnight (one of those stupid traditions). So make sure you say your good-byes early.

THE BACHELOR PARTY (FINAL LECTURE)

I hope you took my advice about the bachelor party and cele-brated a few days before the wedding, but if you didn't, have fun and try to come home at a reasonable hour. Jeez, I sound like your mother now!

THE WEDDING

You have planned for this. It's the big day. Hopefully, you had a good night's sleep.

Wedding-day checklist:

- Wedding license
- Wedding rings
- Honeymoon tickets
- Passport
- Money
- Car keys
- Credit cards
- Bags packed for the honeymoon
- Underwear, socks, shoes, other clothes, bathroom stuff, including the pack of heavy-duty condoms (if necessary)
- Place ice compress on swollen eyes if bachelor party was held the night before

GETTING THERE

Your wedding day is here. You have prepared for months. Now you're ready. Kickoff is at, let's say, 1:00 P.M. If you were the star point guard on the state championship team, would you show up for your basketball game at 1:00 or later? No way. So don't be late to your wedding either. Give yourself plenty of time to get dressed, loosen up, and get to the ceremony. Remember, if you miss the "tip-off" you could be "benched" for life! If you're not proficient in putting on a tux, give yourself extra time to do so. If it takes only fifteen minutes to get to the ceremony location, give yourself thirty. Nothing will frazzle you or your bride more than you showing up late. With the extra time you have made for yourself you can mentally practice reciting your vows or just going through your "moves."

Don't do shots of liquor with your best man in the parking lot to give yourself that extra confidence. Bad move, minus brownie points. A little case of pregame jitters is okay, but if you're not sure about getting married on your wedding day, you're never going to be sure.

Word of warning: If you have a videographer at your wedding he may require you to give your final words as a single man—in other words, a speech. He may also have your best man comment as well. Tell your best man it's not appropriate to mention past girlfriends, the fling you had on spring break, or anything "old lady" related.

THE CEREMONY

Relax. Calm yourself down. Go with the flow. Be flexible. Try to concentrate on what you are supposed to do. If you don't remember something, don't panic. The celebrant, your fiancée, and the best man are there to help you along. Smile. Remember, you will be on camera.

GROOM PLAYING TO THE CROWD

Unfortunately, John (that's me), a big exec
with a high-powered firm, forgot where he was.
During his wedding vows, instead of looking at his bride,
he reverted to his extensive public-speaking training. He
turned to face the crowd and recited his vows to
the congregation instead of to his bride.

MORAL OF THE STORY:
It's about *her*, you idiot, your new bride . . . it's only about *her*.
Don't forget that!

THE RECEPTION

The hard part is over. The reception is your first chance to relax a little—only a little, though, since you and your wife will be pushed, pulled, tugged, grabbed, pinched, yelled at, dragged, and shoved. Make sure your "point man" is available for you at all times. You may feel very confused and disoriented, but that's okay. There will be plenty of people there to tell you what to do and where you are supposed to be.

THE RECEIVING LINE

You're married now. This will be your first formal presentation as Mr. and Mrs. You get to play kissy-kissy with everyone. The receiving line, which can be conducted either directly after the ceremony or at the reception, is where you will get to greet all your guests.

There are many different ways the receiving line can be presented, but typically you and your wife will stand in a line with both sets of parents, and everyone will come to you to give their best wishes. The bridal party may be there with you, or it could just be you, your wife, and the mothers. At some weddings there may not even be a "line." The emcee of the reception, whether that is the bandleader or the DJ, will introduce each person as they enter the room, saving the best for last: you and your wife. You can be certain your wife will tell you well in advance how she would like the receiving line set up.

Receiving lines are horrible; you'll have to stand there and kiss every old lady in the place, even Aunt Bertha with the huge mole on her cheek (the one with gross hair coming out of it). You get to play Mr. and Mrs. Politician. Everyone will wish you well and some may hand you envelopes with money or presents. It's not proper to open the envelopes or presents right there on the spot. Give the handoff to your "point man."

If you opt not to have a receiving line, make sure that you go to every table and greet every guest.

CAKE SMASH

At some point you will be asked to cut the cake with your wife. Humongous minus brownie points if you smash it in her face when she wasn't expecting it. Smushing the cake in her face is childish. My recommendation is that you talk with your fiancée and ask her how she feels about the cake smash before the wedding. Don't arbitrarily smash it in her face hoping she, her family, her friends, and all the rest of the guests will think it's funny. Chances are they will not. Don't turn your wedding into an *Animal House* food fight. Plus, she probably spent a lot of time and money getting a fancy makeup job and you'll end up ruining it with a whole evening of picture taking left.

FIRST DANCE

You will be required to dance. It won't be the Hustle, break dancing, the Lambada, or even the Macarena. You and/or your wife will have picked out a special song just for the two of you. Everyone will be watching, so don't trip. If dancing in front of a lot of people frightens you terribly, concentrate on looking either into your wife's eyes or at her hair. Don't let your eyes wander around the crowd or you will start to freak out. Plus, staring into her eyes will give you mucho brownie points when she watches the video. If you really can't dance, just move your feet back and forth. There isn't much more to it than that.

It's a good idea to try to get in a dance with your mother as well. It can't hurt to earn some brownie points with her too.

THE GARTER

Believe it or not, the garter tradition is supposed to be a chivalrous Prince Charming thing dating back to the Middle Ages and King Arthur's Round Table. The lovely lady in waiting presented her knight in shining armor with a ribbon that he took to battle with him. The English even came up with an official title; kind of like the "Duke of Earl," it's called the "Royal Order of the Garter," and it was an honor given to distinguished noblemen. How in the hell did it disintegrate to its present risqué form?

You know how it works: you sexually assault your new wife in front of the whole congregation by running your hand up under her dress, then throw this little garter thingy to lined-up single guys. The "lucky" guy who catches the garter is then supposed to place it on the thigh of the woman who caught your wife's bouquet. Now, tell me what happens when your frat brother caught the garter and is supposed to place it on the thigh of your wife's ten-year-old cousin? Very tacky. In most states that's enough to get your frat bro arrested! This custom can be fun, but be careful that it doesn't become too burlesque.

PROBLEMS

We talked about this before. Every wedding will have its own set of problems, but what will make your wedding great is that these problems will be handled in an expedient, professional manner. This means that you and your wife won't make a mountain out of a molehill. If the problem happens to be a mountain, such as the cake top-pling over, it means staying calm, thinking the problem through, and reacting effectively. It doesn't mean punching out the caterer. Typically, you and your wife should be sheltered from as many of the glitches as possible. Your "point man" and, to some extent, the bridal party should take care of these problems. If all else fails, improvise.

 Whenever you hear someone say that their wedding was perfect, it just means that their problems were taken care of.

THE FIRST NIGHT

All right, you're married; it's "legal" now to sleep together. This should be the best, most pleasurable night of your life. Yeah, right! After the stress of the long day and being tugged at from all sides, the last thing you feel like doing is consummating the marriage. It's okay if you save it for the honeymoon, a lot of people do. If you do try to "get it on," don't worry if it's not that great—you'll have plenty of time in the future to practice.

I'm assuming that you and your wife aren't virgins and are expe-rienced in the sack. However, if you are virgins, God bless you. If you're not, read on . . .

Some couples try to be cute and "abstain," to revirginize them-selves by not having sex for a month before the wedding. They try to make their first evening as passionate and desirable as possible. This can be great and enhance any sexual relationship. However, I don't know about you, but I wouldn't want to wait a whole month with-out "gettin' any" to have the wedding night arrive and then nothin', because she's tired! Any possible stress relievers will be necessary before the wedding (sex innuendo). As always, talk about it with her and explain your logic. It doesn't mean that she will go for it, but you never know, you might be able to get a quickie, here or there, out of it.

If you feel up to it, you can open the gifts and count the cash before going on your honeymoon. Take your trusty List, and in the gift column write out descriptions of the gifts you received. You're going to need this info when you send thank-you cards.

For extra brownie points:

- After the best man gives his speech, offer to give one yourself
    Thank your parents
    Thank her parents
    Thank all the guests
    Most of all, thank your new wife
- Dance with your mother
- Dance with your grandmothers
- Dance with her mother
- Dance with her grandmothers
- Surprise your wife by sending a bouquet of roses to her home before she leaves for the ceremony
- Send a bouquet of roses to her mother
- Send a bouquet of roses to your mother

CHAPTER 5

HAPPILY EVER AFTER

All the wedding ceremonies in Uzbekistan, Central Asia, take place in September. The men feast, wrestle, and herd goats while the women drink herb tea and eat sweets. During the ceremony, the bride and groom are placed under a blanket together to simulate consummating the marriage. Now that's pressure!

SETTLING INTO MARRIED LIFE

You're back from your honeymoon now and have successfully completed your first "official" extended period of time with your new wife. Hopefully, you didn't get on each other's nerves too much. It wasn't so bad, was it? Now you are back to reality, work, bills, and your in-laws' constant nagging about having kids.

You must now get used to calling her your wife. "I have a wife." She's not your girlfriend anymore. Say it: "my wife." "This is my wife." "Mrs. [fill in the blank]." Not your "ball and chain" or "old lady"; she's your wife. It feels weird saying *wife* and will take time to get used to. As awkward as you feel, she went into the back room to practice writing her new signature.

THE WEDDING VIDEO
AND PHOTO ALBUM

For the next three months be prepared for the new Mrs. to invite any and every person she knows over to your house to watch the video and look at the photographs. The videotape will play over and over, and you will be expected to sit there and view each showing. There is no way out. Expect it. Tolerate it. Make stupid comments. You will find that your other married friends, especially other newly-weds, will rush over to have a look. The girls will be so enthusiastic: "Oh, how beautiful!" Meanwhile, they are all making mental notes about how their wedding was better! The guys, on the other hand, couldn't care less. After you've seen one wedding video and album you have seen enough. Guys, the honeymoon pictures sometimes offer a breath of relief. They tend to be bearable and may provide various rewards for those guys willing to put up with the wedding album. For instance, take out that honeymoon picture you snapped (when your wife wasn't looking) of the topless goddess on that nudie beach in the Caribbean and present your trophy for the other guys to look at.

THANK-YOU CARDS

Within two months of your wedding you should send out thank-you cards to all the people who gave you gifts. If you have kept your trusty List updated, preparing the thank-you cards should be easy. "Tradition" dictates that the gifts and cash you receive are given to your wife or maybe to both of you, but never to just you. This means that technically (I'm reaching here), you don't have to fill out the thank-you cards, since the presents weren't given to you. Okay, guys, I know I'm your hero, and you can thank me now! Major brownie points if you let her know that tradition says that the wife fills out and sends the thank-you cards but add that you, the sensitive and caring husband that you are, would like to assist your wife with the thank-yous as much as possible. Chances are, you will luck out and not have to write some gooey message about how much you just loved that hand-crank can opener from 1946 that Great-Aunt Matilda gave you. But your wife will probably make you fill out the envelopes, stick the stamps, and mail the things.

A NOTE ABOUT GIFTS:

Some of your cheap-ass relatives and friends
may not give you a present right away, or at all.
Wedding etiquette dictates that they can take up to one year
to send a present to you. It is not appropriate for you to
"remind" them that they forgot to give you a gift or for you
to send them that sarcastic thank-you card . . .

To my best friend from high school:
    Thanks a whole hell of a lot for the lovely gift
that you gave us. We really love it and will cherish
it the whole time we are trying to pay off the huge
bar tab and the dinner that you ate . . .
            Sincerely,
            Your ex-friend

FIRST ANNIVERSARY

I know, I know, I'm jumping the gun a little; you're not even
married yet and I'm talking about your first anniversary. Well, it'll
be here before you know it. Each month your wife will diligently
advise you that it's your two-month anniversary, your three-month
anniversary, your four-month anniversary, your five-month anniversary, and on and on. If she doesn't, you can be sure your new
mother-in-law will! For your one-year anniversary, make sure you
do something nice. It should be along the same lines as what you did
for her when you proposed (as long as you took my advice. If not,
reread Chapter 2).

Understanding womanese

If she says:	She means:
You don't have to get me anything for our anniversary.	You better or she will be pissed!
We really can't afford presents, just get me something small.	I expect something small, like jewelry!

Things to expect on your first anniversary:

- Watch the entire ceremony and reception on video
- Look through your photos
- Light the unity candle, if you had one
- Maybe dance to your wedding song
- Eat a stale one-year-old cake
- Give your wife roses
- Give your wife presents
- Maybe get lucky

First anniversaries are strange occurrences. Technically, you are celebrating the first year of your marriage. Why then does it seem as if it's another birthday celebration for your wife?

Here is another "tradition" that has come into "style" over the last ten to twenty years. It goes something like this: On the evening of your first anniversary your wife will pull out the top part of your wedding cake, the same one from your wedding reception. She wrapped it up, all nice and snug, put it in the freezer for a whole year, and, voilà, you have to eat a dry piece of one-year-old stale cake and pretend botulism doesn't affect you, while smiling through the whole process.

HOLIDAYS

Well, you've done it again! Like you didn't have enough problems planning and going through with the wedding. Now you have to deal with the in-laws fighting over where you will spend holidays. I'll tell you right now . . . there is no right answer. No matter what you do, you are going to upset one side of the family. The easiest thing would be to tell everyone to come to your house, but that doesn't always work. So what's the next best thing? Try to divvy up the holidays. One for one. Even Steven.

What you will find is that you will receive subtle but intense pressure to spend the major holidays with your wife's family. There is almost no way around it (unless of course your wife can't stand her family). It's an unwritten law that the wife's family has holiday priority . . . ask your dad and your grandfather. They may tell you no way, but remember when you were a little kid? You went to Grandma's house for holidays, your mother's mother. Settle for any holidays you can get. Take Flag Day and Halloween, because she will get Christmas/Chanukah and Easter/Passover. You may be lucky and get a Fourth of July or Labor Day. Grab it. It may not be available next year. If you're lucky (or unlucky in some cases) and have both sets of in-laws in the same town, it can make holidays easier or much more complicated. Some families will settle for alternating holidays; others take this approach: "You live in the same town and you don't want to see your mother on Memorial Day." The problem is that in-laws are inherently selfish. You agree to visit with both families. The family you visit with first will not let you leave. No matter what you do, as the husband you will be served, along with the roast beef, the guilt treatment. It doesn't matter if the pressure is from your family or hers, as the man of your new house, it's your responsibility to bear the guilt. This phenomena is especially prevalent in Catholic and Jewish families, although it crosses all nationalities, religions, and races.

The picture becomes even more complicated if there are stepparents and stepgrandparents involved.

SEX AND MARRIED BLISS

Unless you're extremely lucky, your sex lives will cease to be what they once were. The majority of the stories that you have heard about "not getting any" are pretty much true. This doesn't mean that your sweetheart doesn't love you as much as she once did. It means the nature of your relationship has changed—you're husband and wife now. It will even get worse when "Junior" arrives. Typically, the lust you experienced while dating may sort of disappear. The stresses of daily life take over, and both of you may find that your passions are subdued. If you are like most guys, you need it all the time. If the sex issue becomes a problem, talk to her about it. I'm not a shrink and I'm not about to lecture you on psychological topics, but you have all heard that communication is the biggest problem in relationships. Most women don't understand the physical needs of men. Most men don't understand the psychological needs of women. Remember, you only get what you ask for. Talk to her about it.

"Until recent times Greek shepherds, newly married, slept in the same unpartitioned hut as the groom's parents, and were required to have permission before engaging in marital intercourse."
—from G. Robina Quale, *A History of Marriage Systems*

When you first started dating you did nice things for her because you wanted too. You brought her flowers, took her out to dinner, surprised her with gifts. Your romance was in full bloom. Why stop now that you are married? Continue to do nice things for her. Ladies like that stuff, they appreciate it, and they may even "reward" you for it (sex innuendo).

There will be problems. No marriage is perfect, and if someone tells you that theirs is, send them for counseling. Always remember why you got married. Never forget that you *wanted* to spend the rest of your lives together and that no one forced you to marry her.

She is your wife, not your mother. Don't expect her to act like your mother either. There is absolutely nothing wrong with helping her around the kitchen or even doing a load of laundry every once in a while. You will be surprised at her reaction if you try helping without her prompting you. Major brownie points.

The husband is feeling frisky and goes to the medicine cabinet. He pulls out two aspirins and gets a glass of water, then walks over and hands them to his wife.
"What's this for?" she says.
"Your headache," he states, very concerned.
"But I don't have a headache."
"All right!!!"
(For you slow guys . . . sex innuendo.)

I wish you good luck with planning your wedding and a married life of happiness!

CHAPTER 6

WORKSHEETS AND RESOURCES

Marriage is like the stock market.
You must continue to invest
to reap the rewards in the future.

GROOM'S TIMELINE TO KICKOFF

First:

- Purchase engagement ring.
- Get engaged.
- Call both sets of parents.
- Discuss with fiancée and then parents a date, time, place, and budget for the wedding.
- Make sure engagement ring is insured.

From fifteen months to six months before kickoff:

- Finalize date, time, place, and budget.
- Start work on the List.
- Determine how many people you and your family can invite and discuss the wedding budget.
- Determine who will pay for what and what you are responsible to pay for.
- Pick best man and groomsmen.
- Do you know where you will be living when you're married? Start planning.
- Find out what the specific requirements are for the ceremony (whether you have to attend classes, meet with a priest, and so on) and add them to the timeline.
- Think about where you want to go on your honeymoon.
- Think about the rehearsal dinner.

- Assist your fiancée in any way possible. Help her finalize her major decisions (reception, photographer, videographer, cake, and the like).

Four months to kickoff:

- Finalize your "A" list.
- Find out marriage-license requirements in the state where you will be married (not where you live).
- Pick out your tux.
- Finalize your honeymoon plans.
- Do you need a passport? Better apply for one now!
- Finalize the rehearsal dinner.
- Finalize accommodations for out-of-town guests and grooms-men, including reserving hotel rooms.
- Book limo.
- Go with your fiancée and take an engagement picture for the newspaper.

Three months to kickoff:

- Purchase wedding bands.
- Send out invitations to "A" list.
- Make sure groomsmen get measured and order their tuxes.
- Select any wedding songs you like.

Two months to kickoff:

- Call all "A" list persons who have not responded.
- Send out your first wave of "B" list invitations.

One month to kickoff:

- Purchase gifts for groomsmen and parents.
- Purchase bride's gift (optional).
- Give list of required pictures to photographer and videographer.
- Confirm hotel reservations for out-of-town guests.

Two weeks to kickoff:

- Get a haircut.
- Square away any change of address if you are moving and arrange for utilities to be turned on at your new place and shut off at your old.
- Make sure you have picked up the wedding bands and that they fit.

One week to kickoff:

- Pick up your tux and try it on to make sure it fits.
- Make sure your groomsmen have picked up their tuxes.
- Reconfirm all honeymoon reservations.
- Have a great bachelor party.
- Pack your honeymoon bags.
- Make sure the marriage license is squared away.
- Make sure you have paid her family any moneys due to them.

Pregame:

- Do you have your honeymoon tickets?
- Marriage license?
- Money?
- Passport?
- Credit cards?
- Try to get some decent sleep.
- Give your "playbook" to the "point man."
- Do you have your tip envelopes ready? Give them to the "point man."

Postgame:

- Send out thank-you cards.

ENGAGEMENT-RING SHOPPING FORM

EXAMPLE

	CARAT	CUT/SHAPE	COLOR	CLARITY	COST	CERTIFIED?	SETTING
Your ultimate diamond	2.00	Ideal/ Marquise	E	IF	$8,000	Yes	Platinum/ $150
Vendor Name Address Telephone Point of Contact							
Artie's Diamonds 1234 Main Street Miami, FL 33000 (305) 555-1234 Mr. Artie Diamond	1.75	Ideal/ Marquise	F	IF	$9,000	No	Platinum/ $150
Gold's Gold 4321 First Street New York, NY 11111 (212) 555-9876 Mr. Joe Gold	1.5	Ideal/ Marquise	E	VSI2	$7,000	Yes	Gold/ $75
The Right Diamond 1 Right Street Washington, DC 22020 (202) 555-3434 Mr. I. M. Right	2.2	Ideal/ Marquise	F	IF	$7,500	Yes	Platinum/ $200

ENGAGEMENT-RING SHOPPING FORM

	CARAT	CUT/SHAPE	COLOR	CLARITY	COST	CERTIFIED?	SETTING
Your ultimate diamond							

Vendor
Name
Address
Telephone
Point of Contact

THE LIST FORMAT

EXAMPLE

"A" LIST

#	NAME ADDRESS TELEPHONE	INVITED TO REHEARSAL DINNER YES–NO	DATE INVITATION SENT	# ATTENDING REHEARSAL DINNER	# ATTENDING WEDDING	GIFT	DATE THANK-YOU CARD SENT
1.	Susan Jones & Guest 123 Main Street Vienna, VA 22042 (703) 555-4567	yes	6/1/99	2	2	Waterford vase	10/2/99
2.	Mr. & Mrs. Mark Smith & Family 456 Elm Street Miami, FL 33065 (305) 555-4321	no	6/1/99	—	4	$100	10/2/99
3.	Tom Thompson 987 First Street Oakton, VA 22043 (703) 555-1234	yes	6/1/99	0	1	$75	10/2/99
4.	Jane Smith & Mike Michael 654 Second Street Miami, FL 33303 (305) 555-4321	no	6/1/99	—	2	$100	10/2/99

Feel free to make as many copies of the List format as necessary. The List format can be used for the "A" and "B" lists.

THE LIST FORMAT

_____ **LIST**

#	NAME ADDRESS TELEPHONE	INVITED TO REHEARSAL DINNER YES–NO	DATE INVITATION SENT	# ATTENDING REHEARSAL DINNER	# ATTENDING WEDDING	GIFT	DATE THANK- YOU CARD SENT

LIST OF EXPENSES

Times change, people change, and, of course, responsibilities for expenses change. I have divided up the expenses into four categories: Groom's family's expenses, Groom's expenses, Bride's family's expenses, and Bride's expenses. This list of expenses should by no means be taken as a hard-and-fast rule. Obviously, there is flexibility for all expenses and who pays for them. In many cases you may have to pay a significant portion of the bills. Typically, any expenses that are either the groom's or the bride's will have to be paid for by you, your bride, or both of you. Some of the expenses may overlap. You will need to sit down and discuss how you will work it out. I can't stress enough how important the money issues will be. Make sure that each party involved—your parents, her parents, your fiancée, and yourself—fully understand, from the beginning, how much they will be required to pay. If you ignore the issue or procrastinate, you may wind up footing the bills yourself and may have pissed off family members to boot.

LIST OF "TRADITIONAL" EXPENSES

Groom's family's expenses:

- Rehearsal dinner
- Tipping the officiant, altar boys, and assistants
- The limo
- The accommodations for your groomsmen
- Boutonnieres for the fathers and groomsmen. (The bride's family will have ordered them. Make sure you reimburse them.)
- Sometimes: bride's bouquet, mothers' and grandmothers' flowers. (The bride's family will have ordered them. Make sure you reimburse them.)

- Sometimes: booze for the reception. (Talk it over with your fiancée.)

Groom's expenses:

- Gifts for the groomsmen
- The engagement ring
- Your tuxedo rental or purchase
- Wedding bands (rings)
- Honeymoon
- Marriage license
- Present for bride (optional)

Bride's family's expenses:

- The reception
- Tips for the reception servers and bartenders
- All other flowers
- Her gown and accessories
- The cake and the groom's cake
- Invitations
- Any music, band, or DJ
- Ceremony fee
- Photographer
- Videographer
- Engagement photo and announcement

Bride's expenses:

- Bridesmaids' gifts
- Thank-you-note stationery
- Wedding video
- Accommodations for the bridesmaids
- Wedding album
- Present for groom (optional)

PHOTOGRAPHER AND VIDEOGRAPHER CHECKLIST

Listed below are some common wedding shots. Check off the ones appropriate for you. Provide copies of this checklist with your selected shots noted, to your photographer and videographer. There is also space at the bottom for your special requests and instructions. Make sure your photographer and your videographer sign separate copies. They should keep a copy, while you should file their originals in your "playbook."

_____ Bride at home

_____ Bride getting into car

_____ Bride getting out of car

_____ Bride coming down aisle

_____ Father giving bride away

_____ Groom and groomsmen at altar (or in procession)

_____ Bridesmaids coming down aisle

_____ Parents coming down aisle

_____ Groom meeting bride at altar

_____ Exchanging vows

_____ The kiss

_____ The lighting of the unity candle

_____ Bride and groom posed on altar

_____ Bride and groom leaving ceremony

Bride with:

_____ groom

_____ her parents

_____ groom's parents

_____ her grandparents

_____ groom's grandparents

_____ best man

_____ maid of honor

_____ wedding party

_____ all relatives (group shot)

_____ friends

Groom with:

_____ bride

_____ his parents

_____ bride's parents

_____ his grandparents

_____ bride's grandparents

_____ best man

_____ maid of honor

_____ wedding party

_____ all relatives (group shot)

_____ friends

_____ Bride and groom arriving at reception

_____ The receiving line

_____ Parents

_____ Grandparents

_____ Stepparents

_____ Other relatives

_____ Friends

_____ Buffet, dessert, and/or cookie table

_____ The cake table

_____ Bride and groom at their table

_____ Head table

_____ Parents' table

_____ Bride and groom cutting cake

_____ Bride and groom feeding each other cake

_____ Bride and groom toasting

_____ Bride and groom's first dance

_____ Bride dancing with her father

_____ Groom dancing with his mother

_____ Bride dancing with father-in-law

_____ Bride dancing with groom's grandfather

_____ Groom dancing with mother-in-law

_____ Groom dancing with bride's grandmother

_____ Best man giving toast

_____ Groom taking off bride's garter

_____ Garter toss

_____ Bouquet toss

_____ Gentleman placing garter on bouquet recipient

_____ Bride and groom leaving reception

Special requests and instructions:

_____

_____

_____

_____

_____

_____

_____   _____

date   (photographer or videographer—circle one)

"RIGHT OF FIRST REFUSAL" PLEDGE

I _____ (groom) and I _____
(bride), being of sound mind and body, hereby agree to the following:

RULES OF THE GAME

1. It is the obligation of the bride to pick the products and services that she wants. The groom will not get in the bride's way or make comments and criticisms to her during her selection process. The groom will give the bride total freedom to plan things her way.

2. Once the bride has made a decision regarding a specific product or service, the bride is required to present the idea to the groom before a contract is finalized with the vendor. The groom has the option of accepting or rejecting the idea. If, and only if, the groom absolutely hates the bride's idea and rejects it outright, it is then the bride's responsibility to go back and reselect. It is the groom's obligation to fully explain to the bride the reason for nonacceptance and, in turn, the groom must offer her alternative ideas. After the bride reselects, the process is repeated and the groom has the right to refuse again.

Special notes:

- Please note that when it is the groom's turn to select a specific product or service the bride has the same "Right of First Refusal."
- The "Right of First Refusal" provides both partners with the ability to stay involved in the wedding planning without aggravating their future spouse too much.
- You should only refuse those things that are utterly disgusting to you. Things that you moderately hate should be accepted.

Remember, your future spouse took a long time and spent a lot of effort to arrive at some of their decisions.

- Plan on having fights but don't let the fight progress to personal attacks against each other. Always communicate.

_____   _____
Groom   Bride

_____   _____
Date   Date

Place the signed copy of the "Right of First Refusal" Pledge in the "playbook."

RESOURCES

WARNING!

**The Surgeon General
warns that calling all these
800 numbers may be hazardous to your health.
You will be placed on untold numbers of mailing lists
and continuously bombarded with travel and other info.
Do not try this at home if you have a weak heart!**

The popularity of the World Wide Web (WWW) and the Internet has grown exponentially. Today there are literally hundreds of sites available for couples who are getting married, offering a virtual treasure trove of information. You can find info on almost any wedding subject that strikes your fancy. Listed below are a few Web sites. By the time you read this book, the whole scope of the Web and the available sites may have changed, so I kept the list short. I have also listed toll-free telephone numbers where applicable for various associations and "info" hot lines. If nothing else, these numbers will enable you to collect a lot of information.

Rings

American Gem Society
(800) 346-8485
http://www.ags.org/about.html

Diamond Promotions Service
(800) 370-6789

Gemological Institute of America (GIA)
(800) 421-7250, ext. 306
http://gia.gia.org/services.html

Jewelers of America
(800) 223–0673

News Groups

alt.wedding

soc.couples.wedding

Other Resources

Association of Bridal Consultants (ABC)
(860) 355–0464

HUD: U.S. Department of Housing and Urban Development (Federal Housing Administration bridal-registry info)
http://www.hud.gov

Office of Passport Services
(202) 647–0518

Honeymoons

Adventure Travel Society
(303) 649–9016

Caribbean and Atlantic Islands

Anguilla
(800) 553–4939

Aruba
(800) 862–7822

http://www.interknowledge.com/aruba

Bahamas
(800) 422–4262

http://www.interknowledge.com/bahamas

Barbados Tourism Authority

(800) 221-9831

Bermuda Department of Tourism

(800) 223-6106

British Virgin Islands

(800) 835-8530

Curaçao

(800) 270-3350

http://www.interknowledge.com/curacao

Grenada

(800) 927-9554

http://www.interknowledge.com/grenada

Jamaica Tourist Board

(800) JAMAICA

http://www.interknowledge.com/jamaica

Nevis and St. Kitts

(800) 582-6208

http://www.interknowledge.com/stkitts-nevis

Puerto Rico Tourist Board

(800) 866-7827

Puerto Rico Tourist Company

(800) 223-6530

Saba

(800) 722-2394

http://www.turq.com/saba

St. Eustatius (Statia)
(800) 722-2394
http://www.turq.com/statia

St. Lucia
(800) 456-3984
http://www.interknowledge.com/st-lucia

St. Martin
(800) 786-2278
http://www.interknowledge.com/st-martin

St. Vincent and the Grenadines
(800) 729-1726

Turks and Caicos
(800) 241-0824
http://www.interknowledge.com/turks-caicos

U.S. Virgin Islands Department of Tourism
(800) 372-USVI

Pacific and Hawaiian Islands

Fiji Visitors Bureau
(800) YEA-FIJI

Hawaii Tourist Information
(888) 547-2612

Mexico and Belize

Belize
(800) 624-0686
http://www.belize.com

Mexican Government Tourism Office
(800) 44–MEXICO

Europe

France
French Government's Tourist Office
(202) 659-7779
http://www.fgtousa.org

Germany
German National Tourist Office
(212) 661-7200

Great Britain
British Tourist Authority
(800) 462-2748
http://www.visitbritain.com

Greece
Greek National Tourist Organization
(212) 421-5777
http://www.compulink.gr/tourism

Italy
Italian Government Travel Board
(212) 245-4822
http://www.visiteurope.com/italy

Continental United States

Pocono Mountains Vacation Bureau
(800) POCONOS

U.S. National Park Service
(202) 208-4747

State Tourist Boards

Alabama
Bureau of Tourism and Travel
(800) ALABAMA

Alaska
Division of Tourism
(907) 465-2010

Arizona
Office of Tourism
(800) 842-8257

Arkansas
Department of Parks and Tourism
(800) NATURAL

California
Division of Tourism
(800) 862-2543

Colorado
Travel and Tourism Authority
(800) COLORADO

Connecticut
Department of Economic Development
(800) CT-BOUND

Delaware
Tourism Office
(800) 441-8846

Florida
Division of Tourism, Visitors' Inquiry
(904) 487-1462

Georgia
Department of Industry, Trade, and Tourism
(800) VISIT-GA

Hawaii
Hawaii Tourist Information
(888) 547-2612

Idaho
Travel Council
(800) 635-7820

Illinois
Bureau of Tourism
(800) 223-0121

Indiana
Department of Commerce, Tourism Division
(800) 759-9191

Iowa
Department of Economic Development, Division of Tourism
(800) 345-4692

Kansas
Department of Commerce and Housing, Travel and Tourism
   Division
(800) 2-KANSAS

Kentucky
Travel Department
(800) 225-TRIP

Louisiana
Office of Tourism
(800) 633-6970

Maine
Publicity Bureau
(800) 533-9595

Maryland
Office of Tourism Development
(800) 543-1036

Massachusetts
Office of Travel and Tourism
(800) 447-MASS

Michigan
Travel Bureau
(800) 5432-YES

Minnesota
Office of Tourism
(800) 657-3700

Mississippi
Division of Tourism
(800) WARMEST

Missouri
Division of Tourism
(800) 877-1234

Montana
Department of Commerce, Travel Montana
(800) VISIT-MT

Nebraska
Division of Travel and Tourism
(800) 228-4307

Nevada
Commission on Tourism
(800) NEVADA-8

New Hampshire
Office of Travel and Tourism
(800) 386-4664

New Jersey
Division of Travel and Tourism
(800) JERSEY-7

New Mexico
Department of Tourism
(800) 545-2040

New York
Convention and Visitors Bureau
(800) NYC-8474 (New York City)
(800) 225-5697 (New York State)

North Carolina
Division of Travel and Tourism
(800) VISIT-NC

North Dakota
Tourism
(800) HELLO-ND

Ohio
Division of Travel and Tourism
(800) BUCKEYE

Oklahoma
Tourism and Recreation
(800) 652-6552

Oregon
Tourism Division
(800) 547-7842

Pennsylvania
Office of Travel and Tourism
(800) VISIT-PA

Rhode Island
Tourism Division
(800) 556-2484

South Carolina
Division of Tourism
(800) 346-3634

South Dakota
Department of Tourism
(800) S-DAKOTA

Tennessee
Department of Tourist Development
(800) 836-6200

Texas
Department of Commerce, Tourism Division
(800) 888-8-TEX

Utah
Travel Council
(800) 200-1160

Vermont
Department of Travel and Tourism
(800) VERMONT

Virginia
Division of Tourism
(800) VISIT-VA

Washington
Division of Tourism
(800) 890-5493

Washington, DC
Convention and Visitors Association
(202) 789-7000

West Virginia
Tourism
(800) CALL-WVA

Wisconsin
Division of Tourism
(800) 432-TRIP

Wyoming
Division of Tourism
(800) 225-5996

BIBLIOGRAPHY

Klock, Frank. *Apes and Husbands.* Alhambra, CA: Borden Publishing Co., 1970.

Quale, G. Robina. *A History Of Marriage Systems.* Westport, CT: Greenwood Press, 1988.

ENGAGEMENT-RING SHOPPING FORM

	CARAT	CUT/SHAPE	COLOR	CLARITY	COST	CERTIFIED?	SETTING
Your ultimate diamond							

Vendor
Name
Address
Telephone
Point of Contact

ENGAGEMENT-RING SHOPPING FORM

	CARAT	CUT/SHAPE	COLOR	CLARITY	COST	CERTIFIED?	SETTING
Your ultimate diamond							

Vendor
Name
Address
Telephone
Point of Contact

THE LIST FORMAT

___ LIST

#	NAME ADDRESS TELEPHONE	INVITED TO REHEARSAL DINNER YES–NO	DATE INVITATION SENT	# ATTENDING REHEARSAL DINNER	# ATTENDING WEDDING	GIFT	DATE THANK-YOU CARD SENT

THE LIST FORMAT

_____ LIST

#	NAME ADDRESS TELEPHONE	INVITED TO REHEARSAL DINNER YES–NO	DATE INVITATION SENT	# ATTENDING REHEARSAL DINNER	# ATTENDING WEDDING	GIFT	DATE THANK-YOU CARD SENT